The Lamb
The Lambkin

Donald A. Peart

The Lamb Copyright © 2005 Donald A. Peart

All rights reserved. This book may be reproduced for noncommercial use for the inclusion of brief quotations in a review, discipleship related teaching, etc. without permission in writing from the author or publisher.

ISBN: 978-1-304-10437-3

Edition: September 2022

DEDICATION

To all the Lamb's kindred who are in heaven and on earth, which also include our five children: Donald Jr. (who designed this book cover), Jeshua, Charity, Benjamin, and Jesse, who are as little lambs in sharing their Mother (Judith) and me with others.

This book is also devoted to all the people of the habitable world who will eventually believe in the Lamb and become partakers of the Kingdom of God.

ACKNOWLEDGMENT

"For it seemed good to the Holy Spirit..." (Acts 15:28a). I also acknowledged all my teacher who have taught me through the years.

HONORS

I would like to honor my wife and friend Judith Peart, my natural parents Lennox Peart and Millicent Peart. I also acknowledge some of those in the ministry (alphabetically) who have been instrumental in my spiritual growth: Apostle Raymond Buie and Pastor Ola Buie, Pastors Steve and Michelle Daniels, Apostle Lewis Sanders, Prophetess Maria Howard, Apostle Sandra Hayden, Apostle Turnel Nelson, Pastor Earl Palmer, Apostle Richard and Prophetess Teresa Scott, Apostle Kelley Varner, Pastor Wendall Ward, and Dr. Samuel Soleyn.

TABLE OF CONTENT

INTRODUCTION – THE LAMB 1
THE LAMB'S BLOOD SPEAKS 5
   JESUS' BLOOD HAS A VOICE 6
   BLOOD GUILT 7
   GOOD CONSCIENCE 10
   BLOOD AND SPIRIT 11
   LAMB … AS IF SLAIN 12
   HEAVEN RECONCILED 14
   THE PRICE OF BLOOD 17
   BLOOD OF THE EVERLASTING COVENANT 19
THE LAMB'S UGLINESS 21
   DISFIGURED APPEARANCE 21
   UGLY ROOT, DRY GROUND 23
   TOO UGLY TO LOOK AT 25
   HIS UGLINESS, OUR PEACE 26
   HE EMBRACES OUR UGLINESS 28
   NO REPRESENTATIVE 29
   BEAUTY 34
   UGLY CIRCUMSTANCES – PRIESTLY COMFORT 37
THE LAMB'S EYES 41
   THOUGHTS CAN BE SEEN 42
   THE WORD HAS EYES 43
   EYES LIKE A FLAME 44
   DOVE'S EYES 46

SEVEN TORCHES 48
LIGHT TO SEE 50
APOSTOLIC EYES 50
THE LAMB'S HEAD 55
    THE ONE HUNDRED AND FORTY-FOUR THOUSAND 57
    SEALED IN THEIR FOREHEAD 62
    SEALED BY THE SPIRIT, THROUGH MAN'S HANDS 65
    SEALED WITH THE INK OF THE SPIRIT 66
THE LAMB'S FEET 69
    LION/LAMB 70
    WISDOM WALK 73
    THE LAMB'S WALK TAKES AWAY SIN(S) 74
THE LAMB'S ENTRAILS 77
    APPROACH BOLDLY 78
    GUT FEELING – COMPASSION 79
    FORGIVENESS FROM THE GUT 80
    COMPASSION FOR FELLOW SLAVES 82
    RESTRICTED IN YOUR BOWELS 85
THE LAMB AND THE OPEN BOOK 92
    BOOK TOWN 93
    OPEN BOOK 96
    APOSTLES OF THE LAMB 99
SILENCED LAMB? 102
    SILENT, BUT NOT SILENCED 102
    SILENT 107

THE LAMB AND THE POOR 111
- THE POOR NEEDS 111
- THE GOSPEL 112
- THE POOR IN SPIRIT 113
- PERFECTED SPIRITS OF MEN AND WOMEN 116
- THE LAMB'S DOMINION 116
- REMEMBERING THE POOR 120
- KINGDOM OF GOD AT HAND 122

THE THRONE OF THE LAMB 125
- NO MORE CURSE 125
- PURE RIVER OF WATER OF LIFE 129
- FRUIT FOR FOOD, LEAVES FOR HEALING 134

THE LAMB'S WIFE 139
- NEW JERUSALEM'S DESCENT 141
- LEAVING MOTHER AND FATHER 142
- JERUSALEM HAVING THE GLORY OF GOD 143
- THE LAMB OF GOD RESURRECTED 145
- INTERNAL PREPARATION 146
- THROUGH MARRIAGE THE BED IS PURIFIED 148

THE LAMB'S FOOD 151
- THE LORD IS FOR FOOD 152
- THE FOOD OF THE WILL OF GOD 154
- THE GOD OF THE BELLY 155
- POWER OF THE HOLY SPIRIT 158
- WHEN WE FAST 160

- **THE LAMB'S WRATH** 163
  - THE SIXTH SEAL 163
  - MOUNTAIN OF DEMONS AND FLESH 167
  - WE SHOULD CRY FATHER, FATHER 168
  - THE LAMB'S DESIRE 170
- **THE LAMB'S SEVEN HORNS** 173
  - SHEARED LAMB 173
  - BORED EYES 176
  - TWO MIDDLE PILLARS DESTROYED 177
  - HORNS OF SALVATION 179
- **LAMBKINS** 183
  - BECOMING 184
  - BE LIKE HIM 185
  - AS HE IS 186
  - GOD'S LIKENESS 187
  - ONE LIKE THE SON OF MAN 190
  - ONE LIKE THE SON OF MAN IN THE SEVEN LAMPSTANDS 191
- **THE LAMB'S LIGHT** 195
  - SUN AND MOON 195
  - THE RAYS OF GOD'S GLORY 197
  - THE LAMB IS THE LIGHT 201
  - THE LIFE IS LIGHT 202
- **THE LAMB IS THE TEMPLE** 205
  - THE PLACE OF WORSHIP 206

    HEART AND HANDS 208
    THE TEMPLE OF JESUS' BODY 211
THE LAMB'S BOOK OF LIFE 212
    WRESTLERS/CO-LABORERS 212
    OVERCOME 213
    DON'T MARVEL AT THE BEAST 216
    ANOTHER BOOK 217
    DO NOT TAKE AWAY 220
THE LAMB, THE ONLY DYNASTY 222
    ONLY FOUR EARTHLY KINGDOMS 223
    THE COLLISION 225
    THE SMITTEN BECAME THE CRUSHER 226
    KING OF KINGS, LORD OF LORDS 228

INTRODUCTION – THE LAMB

Jesus, to me, is the most interesting, and controversial man who has ever walked the earth. The course of mankind has been redirected because of Him. Rome, as an empire, was changed as a result of Him. This is seen in the belief of a Roman emperor, Constantine. In A.D. 313, Constantine established freedom of worship. This eased the centuries of persecution against Christians.

The Lamb of God also caused Constantine to recognize Christianity as a legal body of believers because of his faith in Jesus. In A.D. 391, Christianity became the official religion[1] of Rome. For those with understanding, Constantine, to a degree, exemplified Revelation 11:15 with respect to what God wants to do with all the kingdoms of the earth. Constantine demonstrates that **leaders** have been **changed** – through Jesus – to be a positive impact on their nation. Controversial or not, Jesus is a life changer; and His ultimate goal is "to make **disciples**[2] of **all nations...teaching them** to observe all things that I [Jesus] have commanded..." (Matthew 28:19-20).

---

[1] Please note, there exists understanding that Constantine inviting the Church to be State sponsored has convoluted "Church" to be defined as a manmade building, and representative of respective cultures instead of functioning as the exact representation of Christ which Paul defined to be "the Body of Christ."
[2] Disciples can be defined as not being the general populous of Church buildings attendees but viewed as the various levels of those who followed the Lamb of God closely, the twelve (12), the seventy(70), the one hundred and twenty (120).

Jesus is all that a man or woman will ever need to become the productive **"person"** God intended him/her to be. Jesus is the express image of God's **"person."** In Him all things are held together, including people. He keeps us from falling apart, and for some, Jesus is that bonding agent that holds us together after God reassembles our lives. This is encouraging in a world where people are being shattered every day by both unseen and seen forces.

Jesus is the Lord our Healer; and His tribes are to serve the nations with healing. Thus, one of the purposes of this volume is to impart truth that can help to heal those marred by the corrupt practices, corrupt thinking, corrupt doctrines, and guilt in this present age. This can be accomplished through understanding the "voice" of the Lamb's blood that speaks better things than the bloodguilt that plagues mankind. This text offers the opportunity to be liberated from self-rejection into the acceptance of "how" God created each person to **look**, thus realizing his/her true beauty. Taking a look at Jesus' ugliness will do this.

The Lamb will discuss the Lamb's sight that is like a dove, the Lamb's mind (the mind of Christ), the Lamb's feet (His walk), the Lamb's throne, the Lamb's relation to the poor, and the like. The aim of **The Lamb** is to introduce the **restoration** process towards the right relationship with the Lamb, the Spirit, and God the Father—a **restoration** of the dominion (God's likeness) that Adam fell from.

The Lamb and the Spirit will make the Church **internally** fit. Jesus will do this by empowering the Bride **with** His glory and **in** His glory, as she realizes her freedom from sin, through the blood of the everlasting covenant. Finally, appreciation for the only "Lord" (Jesus) and "King" (Jesus) of the heavens, the earth, and under the earth will also be developed. Jesus is the **"only** Potentate (lit., **only** Dynasty)" that remains.

Jesus is building resilience **in** us, as we prepare ourselves to embrace the Church's dominion in the millennium ("the age") about to be unveiled. Some doctrines of the past have left most of those in the Church world faithless. Fearful of the future (i.e., the beast, which, in reality was already broken by the Stone), they possess no faith to stand in dominion.

Jesus' solution is for the Church to use the Wind (doctrine) of the Holy Spirit to carry away the chaff of the already divided and crushed kingdom of the world. The kingdom of the world must be translated to become the kingdom of our Lord and His Christ. Thus, Jesus' solution is rulership instead of crouching fear. Yet, the attitude of the fearful is the attitude of escapism, being subservient to the world systems and selfishness.

Jesus' tribes should not look for an easy escape out of every difficulty. Jesus' tribes should not allow the world systems to make them passive towards the kingdom of the world. The Church has to be active in maintaining her good confession of rulership in spite of apparent contradictions. Instead of escapism, passiveness and selfishness, Jesus, the Lamb of God, wants the Church to possess His faith and continue to establish God's domain as He exemplified.

Jesus' faith being demonstrated through the Church will be the stabilizer in a deceived world, until all "rule" is put under His and the Church's feet. As Elisha had to endure **seeing** Elijah ascend in the whirlwind to get the reward (the reward of becoming **like** his mentor, by using the same mantle), we must stand faithful, **beholding** the Lamb of God in us as the Church matures to be "like Him." In the words of Hebrews, "We **see** Jesus." Being "like Him" will enable us to lead our lives victoriously until He comes.

Jesus causing His dominion to be **seen** in us is the catalyst for us to become "like Him." In other words, we see who we really are as we see the example of Jesus, the Christ. It will be most glorious for the Church. The "salvation, and the strength and the kingdom of our God and the power (lit.; authority) of His Christ" will be prevalent in and among God's Church.

Therefore, I pray that what you are about to read will encourage you to continue to press into being conformed into **Jesus'** mirror image. I pray that joy instead of sadness, laughter instead of heaviness, an acceptance of who you are instead of rejection of yourself, God consciousness instead of being conscious of self-weaknesses, and faith instead of timidity, may be restored to you. And lastly, I pray the healed and perfected Church will be able to endure and rule in the face of trouble, whether present or future, looking to the joy of the coming Lamb, **Jesus our Messiah.**

THE LAMB'S BLOOD SPEAKS

Hebrews 12:22-24, NKJV:
*22But you have come …24to Jesus …the **blood** of sprinkling that **speaks better** things than that of Abel.*

*Revelation 12:11, NKJV: And they overcame him by **the blood of the Lamb** ….*

Things pertaining to blood—blood of abortion, blood of murder, blood of adultery, blood of incest, blood of not honoring parents, blood of same-sex activity, bloodshed from violence, blood of wars, and even bloodguilt of not preaching the gospel of Jesus are the most critical things among humanity. Bloodshed is such a serious item with the Lord that He judged even the animals for shedding man's blood (Exodus 9:5-6). However, there is relief for the nations from the guilt of bloodshed.

The Lamb of God—Jesus, the Christ—offered His blood for us. This was of utmost importance because "without shedding of blood there is no **remission**" of sins and/or guilt (see Hebrews 9:22). God purchased us with the "price of blood"—**the Lamb's** (1 Corinthians 6:20; 1 Corinthians 7:23; Matthew 27:6; Acts 20:28). The Lamb's blood that was offered for us is a key, because without the blood of Jesus we cannot rid ourselves of our guilt in order to approach God.

The blood of the Lamb is that blood that overcomes the **"voice"** of every bloodguilt that prevents humanity from approaching God. We can only be released to approach God by the strongest blood covenant that was ever ratified. God wants us to hear His voice as we approach Him. He does not want us to be hearing the **voices** of any other blood. You may wonder how this is possible. It is possible because the blood of the Lamb **"speaks** better things" in our conscience. The voice of the blood of Jesus is **"stronger"** than the voice of any other blood.

JESUS' BLOOD HAS A VOICE

*Hebrews 12:22-24, NKJV: ²²But you have come …²⁴ to Jesus the Mediator of the new covenant, and to the **blood** of sprinkling that **speaks better** things than that of Abel.*

*Genesis 4:8-10, NKJV: ⁸Now Cain talked with Abel his brother; and it came to pass, when they were in the field, that Cain rose up against Abel his brother and killed him. ⁹Then the LORD said to Cain, "Where is Abel your brother?" He said, "I do not know. Am I my brother's keeper?" ¹⁰And He said, "What have you done? The **voice** of your brother's **blood cries out** to Me from the ground.*

Jesus came to deliver mankind from the **"voice"** of bloodguilt. There are many in the world tormented by the voice of blood that they have shed on the earth. Some are not even aware of the things that are associated with blood which cause guilt. However, God has remedied that effect of bloodguilt through the voice of a **"better"** blood. Allow me to explain.

I presume that you have heard of the many adverse effects that abortion has on the parents, particularly the mother of the fetus that was terminated. The guilt that is felt by the parents of the fetus, after an abortion is committed, is really the **"voice"** of the baby's blood.

In Genesis 4:8-10, stated above, Cain killed his brother Abel. The Lord then stated that Abel's **"blood [the victim's] cries out."** The same text also stated that blood has a **"voice"** — "the **voice** of your brother's blood cries out to [God]." This is true for any bloodshed — murder, adultery, abortion, hating parents, etc.

The blood of the aborted babies or that of any victim has a voice. We call it guilt. The replay of the feeling of guilt is the voice of the victim's blood crying out for vengeance. The good news is: The blood of the Lamb can overpower the voice of any blood that was shed. (Note: This does not mean that a person is exempt from the legal system if blood is shed against the law. You can be forgiven by God, and still get disciplined by the laws of the land for shedding blood.)

Jesus' **"blood ... speaks better** things than ... Abel." If there is an "Abel" in your history the voice of the blood of Jesus is stronger than the guilt of your conscience. "Better" is the Greek word "**kreítton**" which literally means **"stronger," "to hold."** The root for this word is "**kratos**" which is transliterated as "**great**" in our English language.

The blood of the Lamb is **"greater"** than any bloodguilt we may have. The **voice** of Jesus' blood is **"stronger"** in our conscience than any other voices. In fact, His blood only allows one voice to rule in our heart. That is to say, His blood **"holds"** us to voice of His forgiveness. His blood takes away the consciousness of evil.

One of the reasons why many will not consider serving God is the conscience "accusing" a person with guilt that has been imprinted on their conscience. Some of the bloodguilt on the conscience is not even obvious. However, the guilt is still there. Before I discuss our conscience becoming purged by the Blood of Jesus; let us look at a list of items that generate bloodguilt.

BLOOD GUILT

*Leviticus 20:9, NKJV: For everyone who **curses (lit., make light)** his father or his mother shall surely be put to death. He has **cursed** his father or his mother. **His blood shall be upon him.***

Those who curse his/her father or mother are guilty of blood. In Mark 7:10 "curse" is two Greek words used together, "kakos" (evil or bad) and "logos" (word). This is strong, in light of this generation. We cannot take our parents "lightly" or speak "bad words," regardless of the sins of our parents.

Leviticus 20:11, NKJV: ***The man who lays with his father's wife** has uncovered his father's nakedness; both of them shall surely be put to death. **Their blood shall be upon them.***

This happened in the New Testament (1 Corinthians 5:1). Paul slated the guilty person for death by Satan (1 Corinthians 5:5). The verdict of death was passed by a foundation ministry — an apostle. The point: Sexual immorality is like shedding blood which causes guilt.

*Leviticus 20:12, NKJV: If a man lies with his daughter-in-law, both of them shall surely be put to death. They have committed perversion. **Their blood shall be upon them.***

My wife and I walked a young lady out of a situation like this. Incest can be damaging to both parties. The daughter-in-law and the "man" who initiated the sexual perversion become guilty of blood, especially, if the daughter-in-law is a virgin.

"Their" blood is upon **"them."** The blood guilt of her broken virginity (the hymen) now affects the abused also, hence the plural "their" and "them." Sexual sins are related to blood.

Leviticus 20:13, NKJV: ***If a man lies with a male as he lies with a woman**, both of them have committed an abomination. They shall surely be put to death. **Their blood shall be upon them.***

Blood is also shed during homoerotic acts. The word for covenant according to the Holy Writ means to cut flesh in two pieces where blood flow and then pass between the fleshes. When a man's penis passes through the flesh (hind parts) of another man, an unclean covenant is initiated, and blood covenant is involved through friction. **"Their blood** shall be upon them" — both.

Leviticus 20:15-16, NKJV: *15If a man mates with an animal, he shall surely be put to death, and you shall kill the animal.* *16If a* ***woman approaches any animal and mates with it****, you shall kill the woman and the animal. They shall surely be put to death.* ***Their blood is upon them.***

Bestiality is a crime punishable by death according to God. There is blood guilt involved. For the Church goers, the woman (the apostate Church) who approaches the beast system (Revelation 17:3) is guilty of the blood of Jesus. Man or woman should not sleep with beast/animals naturally or spiritually.

Ezekiel 16:38, NKJV: And I will judge you as women who ***break wedlock or shed blood*** *are judged;* ***I will bring blood upon you*** *in fury and jealousy.*

Breaking wedlock is the same **as** shedding blood. In the word of the prophet Ezekiel, breaking wedlock and shedding blood are equated. Blood will be **brought** upon adulterers by the Lord. Let me say it another way. When a marriage is consummated a blood covenant is established at "marriage sex," even if the couples are not virgins.

Yes, the virgin's hymen in the woman is there for covenant. In addition, every time a man and a woman come together blood is involved. The blood may be in the "micro" dimension, but it is still present. Also, remember the definition I gave earlier for covenant. Blood guilt is involved in adultery.

One can see from the many Scriptures cited in this section, blood guilt ranges from disrespect towards parents to sleeping with an animal. It follows that the conscience of humanity is in a tailspin through the guilt of blood. There are many voices inside the head of humanity crying, "Guilty, guilty."

This is one of the reasons why the blood of Jesus is so important to our conscience. We cannot serve God without our conscience being purged and made good by the blood of the Lamb

GOOD CONSCIENCE

*Hebrews 9:13-14, NKJV: 13For if the blood of bulls and goats and the ashes of a heifer, sprinkling the unclean, sanctifies for the purifying of the flesh, 14how much more shall the **blood of Christ**, who through the **eternal Spirit** offered Himself without spot to God, **cleanse your conscience** from dead works to serve the living God?*

*Hebrews 10:22, NKJV: Let us draw near with a true heart in full assurance of faith, having our **hearts sprinkled from an evil conscience** and our bodies washed with pure water.*

*Revelation 7:14, NKJV: ... "These are the ones who ... washed their robes and made them white in the **blood of the Lamb.***

Your conscience is that voice of guilt that speaks to you when you are alone on your bed at night, thinking on the guilt of your life. It is this consciousness that Jesus' blood can quiet with the sweet voice of His blood that was shed for you and me. Aren't you tired of always feeling bad from guilt—the guilt the Bible calls an "evil conscience," or a "consciousness of evil." We can have a "better" conscience through the blood of Jesus. "Conscience" means "co-perception," or to have two perceptions.

There are two perceptions of evil. A person may believe that he/she is so evil that forgiveness cannot be realized, and at the same time, want to believe that God has indeed forgiven him/her. The consciousness of evil is to believe the former. The consciousness of good is to believe the latter — the blood of Jesus, through the eternal Spirit does indeed deliver from the guilt of sin.

The question is how does a person realize the better blood of Jesus? How do we become conscious of good <u>in lieu</u> of consciousness of evil? Let me begin answering these questions with a question. Have you ever seen the blood of Jesus that was shed 2000 years ago? The answer is no! Yet, we (the Believers in Jesus) claim that the blood of Jesus works today, and it does work today. Therefore, the blood is also **spiritual**. Let me explain.

BLOOD AND SPIRIT

*Hebrews 9:14, NKJV: How much more shall the **blood of Christ**, who through the **eternal Spirit** offered Himself without spot to God, **cleanse your conscience** from dead works to serve the living God?*

*John 6:53-63, NKJV: 54**Whoever eats My flesh and drinks My blood has eternal life,** and I will raise him up at the last day. 55For My flesh is food indeed, and My blood is drink indeed. 56He who eats My flesh and drinks My blood abides in Me, and I in him…. 63It is the Spirit who gives life; the flesh profits nothing. **The words that I speak to you are spirit, and they are life.***

Jesus, before He died, I repeat, before He died, told some of His followers that they had to drink His blood. They thought He was crazy and stopped following Him (John 6:60 w/John 6:66). However, Jesus knew exactly what He was talking about, and gave the explanation.

"It is the Spirit who gives life; the flesh profits nothing. **The words that I speak to you are spirit, and they are life.** Before He died, He linked the Holy Spirit to His blood and body. They could drink His blood through the Holy Spirit. The blood of Jesus is related to the Spirit of the Lord.

Hebrews 9:14, quoted above, states that the blood of Jesus is linked to the **"eternal Spirit."** This is one of the reasons why the blood is as potent in the conscience today as it was on the day He was crucified. In fact, He was slain before the world was created. Therefore, the followers in John, Chapter 6, could appropriate the blood of the Lamb through the Holy Spirit.

1 Peter 1:19-20, NKJV: *19but with* **the precious blood of Christ, as of a lamb** *without blemish and without spot.* *20***He indeed was foreordained before the foundation of the world,** *but was manifest in these last times for you*

Revelation 13:8, NKJV: All who dwell on the earth will worship him, whose names have not been written in the Book of Life of **the Lamb slain from the foundation** *of the world.*

The same is true today. The blood of Jesus can be applied to the conscience through the eternal Spirit. In other words, the sacrifice of Jesus is as fresh as it was approximately two thousand years ago. His blood that was shed for us is always **"new"** and His blood is full of life. His blood is **"living;"** and His blood applied to our conscience causes us to "serve the **living** God."

LAMB ... AS IF SLAIN

Hebrews 10:19-20, NKJV: *19Therefore, brethren, having boldness to enter the Holiest by the blood of Jesus,* *20by a* ***new*** *and living way which He consecrated for us, through the veil, that is, His flesh*

According to Vines Expository Dictionary, the word **"new"** in verse 20 above **(Greek, prosphatos)**, originally signified "**freshly slain.**" Jesus is the **"recently"** slain sacrifice for every age. Before I lose you, He was only slain the day before yesterday.

One day with the Lord is as a thousand (2 Peter 3:8). Two thousand years ago is the day before yesterday to God. In addition, He is freshly (recently) slain because one of His omnipresent manifestations is **"as"** a slain Lamb.

Revelation 5:6, NKJV: And I looked, and behold, in the midst of the throne and of the four living creatures, and in the midst of the elders, stood a Lamb as though it had been slain...

*Revelation 5:6, NASU: And I saw between the throne (with the four living creatures) and the elders a Lamb standing, **as if** slain...*

The Scripture is the authority. It cannot be denied. This is one of the Lamb's omnipresent manifestations. Proof: The Lamb was in more than one place at the same time, in the verse stated above. He was "in the midst of the throne." At the same time, He was in the "midst ... of the four living creatures." In addition, He was also "in the midst ...of the elders." The Lamb was omnipresent in the middle of all the entities listed above, plus more.

The omnipresent Lamb is on His throne (Revelation 3:21). He is in us—His Church (Colossians 1:27). "The Lord is the Spirit" (2 Corinthians 3:17), etc. The Lord is everywhere being all who He is to everyone—He is omnipresent.

It follows that one of His omnipresent manifestations is that of **"Lamb ... as if slain."** Thus, His blood and sacrifice is as fresh today as it was the day before yesterday. This truth is made experiential through the eternal Spirit. The blood of the Lamb is linked to the Spirit of the Lord. As it is written: "...the **blood of Christ**, who through the **eternal Spirit** offered Himself without spot to God, **cleanses your conscience** from dead works to serve the living God" (Hebrews 9:14)?

The blood of the Lamb speaks in such a way that our conscience can be conscious of the good words of the blood of Jesus, as opposed to the bad words of the blood of guilt. The blood of the

Lamb reconciled us to hear the good words out of heaven again, in this life.

HEAVEN RECONCILED

Colossians 1:19-20, NKJV:[19]For it pleased the Father that in Him all the fullness should dwell, [20]and by Him to **reconcile all things** *to Himself, by Him, whether things on earth or* **things in heaven,** *having made* **peace through the blood** *of His cross.*

Soon after the Lord's blood brought me into fellowship with Him again, I read this verse. After reading it, I questioned why the blood of Jesus had to reconcile "things in heaven." It did not make sense to me because Adam sinned on the earth, so I thought. Adam did sin on the earth. However, that is not completely true. The fact is, Adam sinned in heaven. Thus, the heavens had to be reconciled. Let me explain!

2 Corinthians 12:2-4, NKJV: [2]I know a man in Christ who fourteen years ago--whether in the body I do not know, or whether out of the body I do not know, God knows--such a one was caught up to **the third heaven.** *[3]And I know such a man--whether in the body or out of the body I do not know, God knows – [4]how he was caught up into* **Paradise** *...*

Paul called "the third heaven" "Paradise." This is pretty straightforward. The next question is, "What is Paradise?" According to Jesus, through the apostle whom the Lord loves, Paradise is the place where the tree of life exists.

Revelation 2:7, NKJV: He who has an ear, let him hear what the Spirit says to the churches. To him who overcomes I will give to eat from **the tree of life,** *which is in the midst of the* **Paradise of God.**

Paradise is "the third heaven." The tree of life is in the "Paradise of God." We also know that this same tree of life is in the middle of the Garden of Eden (Genesis 2:8-9; 3:22-23, etc.). Therefore, Paradise is the Garden of Eden, which is the third heaven.

Adam sinned in the Garden of Eden. Therefore, **Adam sinned in heaven**. The first sin by Adam was committed in heaven (Genesis 3). Therefore, Jesus' blood had to also reconcile the things in heaven. The logical question is: if Adam sinned in heaven, how did sin get on the earth?

*Genesis 2:15, NKJV: Then the LORD God **took** the man and **put him in the garden of Eden** to tend and keep it.*

*Genesis 3:22-23, NKJV: ²²Then the LORD God said, "Behold, the man has become like one of Us, to know good and evil. And now, lest he put out his hand and take also of the tree of life, and eat, and live forever" – ²³therefore the LORD God **sent (lit., to drive out, to divorce)** him out of the garden of Eden to till the ground from which he was taken.*

Genesis 2:15 establishes the truth that Adam was **taken** and **"put in the garden of Eden."** The word "took" when referenced by the writer of Hebrews means Adam was "translated" into the Garden of Eden, which is the third heaven. After he sinned in the third heaven, He was then "driven out" of the third heaven—Eden. Thus, "sin entered the world" through Adam, after he was driven out of the third (world) of heaven.

*Romans 5:12, NKJV: Therefore, just as **through one man sin entered the world**....*

My point is that the Lord had to reconcile the things in heaven because that is where the first Adam and the devil sinned. I call this "sin in the spirit." It is a serious thing when anyone sins in the spirit, as opposed to sinning in the earth. Whenever a person sins in the spirit (which is heaven, Revelation 4:1-2) a person can lose his/her ability to eat of the tree of life.

This may be a reason there are so many dead Christians. This may be the reason so many are trying through emotional ecstasy to go to heaven because they were kicked out for sinning in the spirit. The blood of the Lamb is the only way to be reconciled to the heavenly dimensions.

God sent His Son to "**reconcile all things ... things in heaven,** having made **peace through the blood** of His cross." We now sit with Jesus in heaven with the Lord in peace through the Lamb's blood.

Ephesians 2:3-6, NKJV: *⁴But God, who is rich in mercy ... made us alive together with Christ...⁶and raised us up together, and made us sit together in the **heavenly places** in Christ Jesus*

Colossians 1:19-20, NKJV: *¹⁹For it pleased the Father that ... by Him to **reconcile all things** to Himself, by Him, whether things on earth or **things in heaven,** having made **peace through the blood of His cross.***

Just like the first Adam was taken to the Paradise of God, so likewise, we now sit together in the heavenly places in Christ. There is a key though. You must be in Christ—Head and Body (1 Corinthians 12:12). This is only done "through the blood of His cross." One of the purposes of this heavenly reconciliation is that we can hear the good words of God in our conscience again.

Ephesians 1:3, NKJV: ***Blessed (Gk., eulogetos)*** *be the God and Father of our Lord Jesus Christ, who has **blessed (Gk., eulogeo)** us with every spiritual blessing **(Gk., eulogia)** in the heavenly places in Christ*

"Blessed" and "blessing" is a combination of two Greek words— **"eu"** (good or well) and **"logos"** (words or expressed thoughts). We get our English word eulogy from this Greek compound. Eulogy means to speak well over. Remember, earlier in this chapter we showed that the blood of the Lamb speaks "better things."

These eulogies are made real by the blood of the Lamb. The heavenly places **in** Christ, through His blood, speak better and good things over us. Here is a good word from the blood of the Lamb—the Lord did not die for you to make you valuable. On the contrary, He paid the price of blood for you because you **are indeed** valuable.

THE PRICE OF BLOOD

Matthew 27:3-8, NKJV: *³Then Judas, His betrayer, seeing that He had been condemned... brought back the **thirty pieces of silver** to the chief priests and elders, ⁴... And they said, "What is that to us? You see to it!" ⁵Then he threw down the pieces of silver in the temple ... ⁶But the chief priests ... said, "It is not lawful to put them into the treasury, because they are **the price of blood."** ⁷And they consulted together and bought with them the **potter's field....** ⁸Therefore that field has been called the **Field of Blood** to this day.*

1 Corinthians 6:20, NKJV: ***For you were bought at a price;*** *therefore, glorify God in your body and in your spirit, which are God's.*

There is a lot in the verses above. He was sold for thirty pieces of silver. However, it actually "cost" more than that for our salvaging. The Scripture aptly called the "cost" for salvaging us "the price of blood." The price is "thirty pieces of silver.

This is what the Zechariah 11:9-13 calls a "goodly price" (KJV) or a "princely price" (NKJV). The Hebrew definitions for "goodly" or "princely" are amplitude, mantle, expand, great, splendor (see Strong's Concordance). **"Mantle"** points to His blood that covers us. His blood is that **"great"** price. The Lord gives us **"splendor"** through the blood of His Son. The Church is to **"expand"** the Church of the living God, through the blood of the cross.

Finally, the **blood speaks** with an **"amplitude"** that is heard in every creature. The "price" is the blood of God's equal (Jesus), which is also called the "price of blood." **God in the flesh** died for us. We were so valuable to God that **"God manifested in the flesh"** and died for us.

1Timothy 3:16, NKJV: *"And without controversy great is the mystery of godliness:* **God** *was manifested in* **the flesh,** *justified in the Spirit, seen by angels, preached among the Gentiles, believed on in the world, received up in glory.*

God birthed Himself in the form of His Son Jesus (see also John 1:18, NAU). God manifested Himself in the flesh to shed His blood for us. He did not only die for us to make us valuable; He died for us because we are valuable. We are that "treasure" that was "hidden in a field" that was worth "all that He [the Lord] has" (Matthew 13:44).

The value of humans was the price of His blood. This is the value the Lord placed on you and me (the value of His very own blood). "For you [us] were bought at a price." His betrayal money was also used to buy the "potter's field" – the "Field of Blood." Jesus said, "the **field** is the **world**" (Matthew 13:38).

The world is a field of blood. Everyone seems to be selling out those whom they do not like. Murder, rape, drug dealing, sexual sins, and the like are prevalent in these times; and it takes the blood of the Lamb to redeem the field of the world that is "struggling" in its own bloodshed (Ezekiel 16:6) and make it a potters' field.

In other words, the Lord is using His blood to redeem those who are guilty of blood. He is then molding the "field" of the world as the potter because He is the Potter (Jeremiah 18:4-11). It took the sweat of God to redeem the World. He resisted sin to the point where blood flowed – the blood of the everlasting covenant.

BLOOD OF THE EVERLASTING COVENANT

*Hebrews 13:20, NKJV: Now may the God of peace who brought up our Lord Jesus from the dead, that great Shepherd of the sheep, through the **blood of the everlasting covenant***

*Luke 22:44, NKJV: And being in agony, He prayed more earnestly. Then **His sweat became like great drops of blood** falling down to the ground.*

*Hebrews 12:4, NKJV: You have not yet resisted to **bloodshed**, striving against sin.*

Something **"everlasting"** was established with the blood of Jesus. It is an "everlasting **covenant."** Jesus prayed so earnestly against sin that His sweat became blood. He strove against sin to the point of bloodshed, before He got abused with beatings, and before blood flowed on the cross. He strove against the sin of mankind in the Garden. Adam sinned in a Garden. Jesus overcame sin in a garden, and He was crucified near a garden (John 18:1; John 19:41).

It was in the Garden of Eden that the Lord said that the curse of "sweat" would be upon Adam for Adam's transgression. It follows that it was in a garden that the Last Adam (Jesus) took on that curse of "sweat" and demolished that curse forever. There is a new covenant. It is **"everlasting"** through the blood of Jesus. We are free from the curse of a nonproductive **earth. "…The profit of the land is for all…" (Ecclesiastes 5:9).** The land must now yield her strength for the children of God (contrast Genesis 4:12 which was implemented because of bloodshed).

Genesis 3:17-19, NKJV: [17] *Then to Adam He said, "Because you have heeded the voice of your wife and have eaten from the tree of which I commanded you, saying, 'You shall not eat of it':* **"Cursed** *is the* **ground** *for your sake; in toil you shall eat of it all the days of your life.* [18] *Both* *thorns and thistles it shall bring forth for you, and you shall eat the herb of the field.* ¹⁹ **In the sweat of your face you shall eat bread** *till you return to the ground, for out of it you were taken; for dust you are, and to dust you shall return."*

The ground was cursed because of Adam's sin. It would take his "sweat" to eat bread from the precious earth. The Septuagint (Greek) translation of the Old Testament of this word "sweat" is the same Greek word used by Luke concerning the "sweat" of Jesus that became "as 'clots' of blood." The link is that the blood-sweat of Jesus redeemed the earth (land) and us from any curse (compare Galatians 3:13; Revelation 22:3). We now have an everlasting covenant which makes us free from the sweat of sin and the sweat of providing for our daily provisions. We "overcame ... by the **blood** of the Lamb" (Revelation 12:11).

THE LAMB'S UGLINESS

Isaiah 52:14, NKJV: ***Just as*** *many were astonished at you,* ***so His visage was marred more than any man,*** *And His form more than the sons of men*

Jesus Christ (the Lamb of God) is the ugliest man God ever made. Yes! There is none as ugly as He, neither will there be any created as ugly. I know, for some, this is hard to believe. Some may also say, "I thought Jesus has blond hair and blue eyes." Or some may say, "Jesus is black, with Jamaican dreadlocks."

The answer to both of these statements is **no.** Jesus, the Christ, is none of the above. Jesus is the ugliest man God ever made. Let us look at the Scripture stated above for an understanding.

DISFIGURED APPEARANCE

In Isaiah 52:14, the Lord says, "Just as many were astonished at **you,** so His visage was marred more than any man." **"You"** who? "You" Isaiah! The verse is saying, Isaiah, Just **as** many were stunned at you, "So **His** visage (lit.., His beauty) was marred more than any man." The **"His"** in this part of the verse refers to **Jesus, the Lamb of God.** Traditionally, the elders taught that the **marring** took place during the time of His capture up to His crucifixion. This is true, but not complete.

To completely understand the full truth of this Scripture, it must be fully interpreted. The verse above can be interpreted as follows: Just as many were stunned at Isaiah's visage (beauty, appearance), so will "many" be stunned at "His" (Jesus') appearance. According to the Scripture, Isaiah was an ugly man.

Isaiah was so ugly that people were stunned at his appearance. And, by the way, the people of his day saw Isaiah's body; and, from reading the Scripture, Isaiah's body was not a pretty sight.

Isaiah 20:2-3, NKJV: ²At the same time the LORD spoke by Isaiah the son of Amoz, saying, "Go, and remove the sackcloth from your body, and take your sandals off your feet." **And he did so, walking naked and barefoot.** ³Then the LORD said, "**Just as** My servant Isaiah has walked naked and barefoot **three years** for a sign and a wonder against Egypt and Ethiopia; so, shall the king of Assyria lead away the Egyptian prisoners.

The lord used the words **"just as"** again to Isaiah when He indicated to Isaiah that his ugliness was foreshadowing Christ's ugliness. **"Just as** many were astonished at **you...."** When were they astonished at Isaiah? **"Just as"** the three years he "walked naked and barefoot"

Yes! For three years he walked naked, and they saw his deformed body. Therefore, not only did Isaiah's words point to the Messiah, but his very bodily shape was also representative to a degree of Jesus' ugliness. Isaiah was not a pretty sight to look at.

Thus, the people were also stunned at Jesus' ugliness. This happened before His Passion, as you can see. Why were they stunned at the Lord's appearance? The answer is the Lord's appearance "was marred (lit., disfigured) more than **any** man." Jesus' **visage (lit., face, beauty, appearance)** was disfigured more than any man. Do you see it? Listen to the rest of the verse, "and his form (lit., outline, delineation) **more than** the sons of men."

The Lamb's outline (bodily shape) was **"more"** deformed than any son or daughter of men to ever be birthed on this earth. As stated above, His outline (His bodily appearance) is disfigured **"more than"** any man who will ever exist. This includes His face, His build, His arms, His legs, and every other physical part of Him. The Scripture teaches that there is a reason for this truth, as you will see later. However, let me look at this truth from some other verses.

UGLY ROOT, DRY GROUND

*Isaiah 53:2, NKJV: For He shall grow up before Him as a tender plant, and as a root out of dry ground. He has no **form** or **comeliness**; and when we see Him, there is no beauty that we should desire Him.*

We see here the Lord is symbolically called a "root" that came out of "dry ground." This is significant, especially if one looks at it allegorically. First, one must note as stated above, the word "root" is **representative** of the man, Jesus. Therefore, the words "dry ground" can also be a representation or symbol if one is to be consistent. To see this point of view (understanding) clearly, let us look in the book of beginnings (Genesis) for the interpretation.

Genesis 2:6-7, NKJV: [6] ***But*** *a mist went up from the earth and watered **(lit., to quaff — to drink deeply, to guzzle)** the whole face of the ground.* [7] ***And** the LORD God formed man of the **dust (or mud)** of the ground and breathed into his nostrils the breath of life; and man became a living being.*

First, **the word "But"** in verse six is the same Hebrew prefix translated **"And"** in verse seven. Therefore, verse six is not a contrast to verse seven, but a continuation. Also, you can logically see that the action of verse seven took place after the action of verse six. Now, let us look at these verses a little more deeply.

The Lord caused the earth to be **"watered"** or "to drink water deeply." So, the man came out of **"deep"** dirt (compare Ps. 42:7). Thus, the water, from the mist, moistened the earth. He wanted the dry earth to become wet ground (mud). In the words of the King James Version, the earth was "watered."

It was from the "watered" (or moist) ground that the Lord **formed** Adam. Do you see it? Look at the order again; the water from the mist (cloud or fog) watered the earth. **"Afterwards,"** "the Lord God formed (lit., to mold, or shape by squeezing) man of the **dust** (lit., mud) of the ground."

The word **dust** in verse seven also means **mud,** according to Strong's Concordance, # 6083. This is a solid definition because of what happened in Genesis 2:6. Water mixed with dirt equals mud. This enabled God to shape, mold and beautify Adam into the proper figure He wanted. Any vessel, on a potter's wheel can easily be worked into any shape if the clay is moist. God was that Potter with Adam and Jesus.

However, Jesus was molded in the hand of "the Potter" from "dry ground." This "molding" from dry ground is seen allegorically of how the root (Jesus) grew up out of the dry ground, according to Isaiah. **A root, in a dry (parched) ground, is discolored and ugly.** The dry ground points to the fact that **Jesus was not formed beautifully,** as was the first Adam.

In other words, it is difficult, if not impossible with man, not God, to mold or shape dry dirt. God formed Jesus out of dry ground. Therefore, our Lord had "no form or comeliness" (Isaiah 53:2, NKJV). He had "no form;" because, it is difficult to mold dry ground into a particular form. On the other hand, wet dirt, or clay in the hand of a potter can easily be beautified. Do you see it?

The fact that our Lord came out of dry ground is the reason the rest of the same verse (Isaiah 53:2) says, "And when we see Him, There is no beauty that we should desire Him" (Isaiah 53:2). This demonstrates that Jesus is the ugliest man God ever made, which compliments Isaiah 52:14 beautifully. In fact, He was so ugly that men rejected Him.

TOO UGLY TO LOOK AT

Isaiah 53:3, NKJV: He is despised and rejected by men, a Man of sorrows and acquainted with grief. **And we hid, as it were, our faces from Him;** *He was despised, and we did not esteem Him.*

One can see from this verse, that our Lord Jesus was rejected and despised. Those who saw Him hid their faces from Him. One of the reasons for men hiding their faces from Him was Jesus' ugliness. We learned this earlier from Isaiah 52:14, and Isaiah 53:2. "Why is this so important brother Peart?" Hold on a little, I will explain soon.

Jesus was so ugly bodily that sometimes men could not bear to look at Him. Listen to my interpretation: "And we hid, as it were, our faces from Him (because of his ugliness); He was despised (because of His ugliness), and we did not esteem Him (because of His ugliness)." Man! Can one imagine the pain Jesus felt when men rejected Him! Why did they do it? **He was too ugly to look at!** Let me tell an event.

This event happened to me, at a time in my life when I was struggling with my own self-esteem. After I got out the Marine Corps, I became so dirt poor that I began even to hate myself. In fact, God used this situation to help heal my mind. In my mind, I was treating people the way I felt about myself. Therefore, God used the situation to heal me. Thus, I can now help someone else. The event took place my first year in Engineering School.

One day, while waiting for class to begin, a young man (an angel, Hebrews 13:1) came to me for direction. The man was so disfigured in the face that it was difficult to look at him. I was so stunned (compare Isaiah 52:14) at his disfigurement that I did not want to talk to him. I did not even want to be associated with him. Because of these inner feelings, I began to cry within, holding back the tears without.

I felt, in my heart that I had denied the Lord. The reason this denial was so disturbing to me was the Lord had taught me about Jesus' ugliness the night before I met this young man. Thus, I fulfilled the Scripture in Isaiah 53:3, "And **we** hid as it were our faces from Him...." Yes, all of **"we"** (us) have denied the Lord's ugliness.

All of "we" are sometimes still ashamed of Him. If anyone does not believe that we **all** denied Him (His ugliness), take a look at the pictures of Jesus men and women have on their walls. Some have Him portrayed as a handsome Black man, or a good-looking white man. These pictures deny the true look of Jesus' ugliness.

Nonetheless, I did embrace the young man's disfigurement, and I helped him. In helping him, I embraced myself. But the idea that I had denied the Lord's ugliness was painful. My mind flashed back to the Scriptures (I was searching for how Jesus must have felt). I realized He was "a man of sorrows" (Isaiah 53:3; 2 Corinthians 6:10).

The young man was an angel sent by God. This is because he was a **stranger** to the school campus. I never saw him again on campus or off campus (compare Hebrews 13:1). He was sent to test and heal my acceptance of Jesus' ugliness. Thus, once I embraced the Messiah's ugliness, I was able to embrace myself and my impoverished circumstances at that time. The Scripture says He carried our sorrows. Therefore, He could identify with my feelings and give me peace.

HIS UGLINESS, OUR PEACE

Isaiah 53:4, NKJV: Surely, He has borne our griefs and carried our sorrows; yet we esteemed Him stricken, smitten by God, and afflicted.

Isaiah 53:5, NKJV: But He was wounded for our transgressions, He was bruised for our iniquities; **the chastisement for our peace was upon Him,** *and by His stripes we are healed.*

These verses are highlights of Jesus' sufferings while upon the earth, including, but not limited to, the cross. Yet, if one will note: He was ordained to suffer before the foundation of the world (1 Peter 1:20). The Book of Revelation, Chapter 13 says, He was a "Lamb slain (or maimed) from the foundation of the world."

Therefore, one can see truth in Isaiah 53:4, concerning things that happened in the **invisible, which** were manifested in the visible, almost two thousand years ago. My point is this: He was also made with "the chastisement for our peace upon Him." In the text above, Jesus carried our grief and sorrows. According to the subject of this chapter, the sorrows He carried include, but not limited to, the sorrow of ugliness, or self-esteem problems.

That is, He heard and carried the way people felt about His disfigurement. His ugliness was so mind boggling, people thought Him to be plagued, smitten, and cursed by God (see Isaiah 53:4 above). "But he was wounded (Rev. 13:8) for our transgression, he was bruised (Rev. 13:8) for our iniquities: the chastisement of our peace was upon him; and with his stripes we are healed" (Isaiah 53:5).

We can have peace in our ugliness because the chastisement of our peace was upon Him, bodily. He can heal anyone who feels ugly or has low self-esteem. Remember, Jesus, Himself was not esteemed by men (Isaiah 53:4). **He was smitten (i.e., made ugly by God, for our healing).** It is written, "And by His stripes we are healed" (Isaiah 53:4). The Scripture also says, **"Surely He** has borne our griefs, and **carried our sorrows...."**

Yes, this speaks of the sorrow of ugliness, which plagues mankind, and the sorrow of self-esteems problems that cause people to become promiscuous just to be accepted. Jesus can heal you and give you peace about your self-worth. He felt what sorrows anyone would ever feel.

Therefore, he can **"sympathize"** with our weakness (Hebrews 4:15, NKJV, NIV). He can be **"touched"** (KJV) with what you feel. There is a real and living flesh and **bone** Jesus in heaven (Luke 24:39-41). He is not a spirit who has not felt your pain. So, reach out and **"touch Him"** (compare John 20:25-27).

HE EMBRACES OUR UGLINESS

*Hebrews 4:15, KJV: For we have not a high priest which cannot be **touched** with the feelings of **our infirmities;** but was in all points tempted like as we are, yet without sin.*

*Hebrews 4:15, NKJV: For we do not have a High Priest who cannot **sympathize** with our weaknesses, but was in all points tempted as we are, yet without sin.*

Jesus, our High Priest, can be **touched** with the feelings of "our infirmities" (lit., our weaknesses). Anyone who feels the Lord made him/her ugly (according to today's standards), remember, God made Jesus uglier (Isaiah 52:14b). Therefore, He can be "touched," or He can sympathize with our ugliness. The word "touched" is translated "sympathetic." Thus, He is sympathetic towards all.

Jesus will let every individual know they are beautiful, compared to Him. He is able to aid (comfort) them that are tempted (Hebrews 2:18). Jesus was in **"all points** tempted as we are" (Hebrews 4:15). This means, He was also tempted in the area of self-esteem. So, smile, and feel good about yourself. Jesus is our peace because **he embraces our ugliness.**

When I was living in North Carolina in the early 1990s, I was the teacher for a cell group; and because this understanding of Jesus' ugliness was so real to me, I taught it immediately. As I was relaying this word from God, a lady who was visiting the area began to cry. I stopped and asked her, "Why are you crying?" She replied by stating that her son went to a particular church on a Sunday after being released from jail (her son at the time also had dread locks).

The lady continued by saying that the Church kicked her son out of the fellowship and called him "ugly" because he had dreadlocks, and he was Black. As she continued to weep, she indicated how the word had blessed her. She also said she would tell her son about the good news of Jesus who accepted her son's ugliness. As stated above, Jesus is our peace, **because He embraces our ugliness** — "the chastisement for our peace upon Him."

Remember, Jesus is not blond haired, or blue eyed. Neither is he a handsome Black man with dread locks. He is a Jew. He is the ugliest man God ever made. No one is able to draw a true representation of our Lord. First of all, **we were not there** when He walked the earth. Most importantly, the Scripture teaches that there is no representation of Jesus. **None can look like Him because He is one of a kind.**

NO REPRESENTATIVE

*Isaiah 53:2, NKJV: For He shall grow up before Him as a tender plant, And as a root out of dry ground. He has no **form** (**lit., representation**) or comeliness; and when we see Him, there is no beauty that we should desire Him.*

There is "**no representation**" for Jesus; yet men like to draw handsome pictures of Jesus. In Ezekiel's day, Israel also worshipped pictures of men portrayed on walls. These were images of the Chaldean (Babylonian) men. The Israelites loved to worship the beauty of men (Isaiah 43:13), rather than the living God. So, likewise, in our day, people gloat over outward beauty. This kind of attitude creates whoredom in people.

Ezekiel 23:14-15, NKJV: ¹⁴*But she increased her harlotry; she looked at* **men portrayed on the wall,** *Images of Chaldeans portrayed in vermilion,* ¹⁵*Girded with belts around their waists, Flowing turbans on their heads, all of them* **looking like captains,** *In the manner of the* **Babylonians** *of Chaldea, the land of their nativity.*

The children of Israel worshipped the pictures of men upon the walls of Babylon. They were "princes (lit.; generals) to look to" (KJV), or "looking like captains [lit.; generals (NKJV)]" meaning they were handsome pictures to look at, like a man in military outfit. So likewise, **Mystery Babylon** (apostate religion, Revelation17:1-5) has made beautiful and false images of **their** Jesus — which is "another Jesus."

Babylon does claim to have "the light of a lamp" and the "voice of the bridegroom" — Jesus (Revelation 18:23). However, this "voice" and "light" is not the true representation. According to Paul, some do preach "another Jesus" and "a different gospel" (2 Corinthians 11:4). In other words, the modern images of Jesus are not necessarily scriptural; yet leaders have these man made images all over the place.

These modern images of **their** Jesus are "portrayed on the wall" — the wall(s) of Churches, and homes, giving a false representation of Jesus. Some in the Church are worshipping these beautiful Babylonian images. Ezekiel says, "She (some in the Church) increased her harlotry." Images of the Black Jesus and the White

Jesus are wrong. These images are made after corruptible man (Romans1:23). In fact, the Lord commands us not to corrupt His image by making images (i.e., pictures and statues).

Deuteronomy 4:15-16, KJV: ¹⁵*Take you therefore good heed unto yourself, for you saw no manner of similitude on the day that the Lord spoke unto you in Horeb out of the midst of fire.* ¹⁶**Lest you corrupt yourselves,** *and make you a graven image, the similitude of any figure, the likeness of male and female.*

Deuteronomy 4:15-16, NKJV: ¹⁵*"Take careful heed to yourselves, for you saw no form when the LORD spoke to you at Horeb out of the midst of the fire,* ¹⁶**lest you act corruptly** *and make for yourselves a carved image in the form of any figure: the likeness of male or female."*

We are warned not to pursue to **know** Jesus according to His fleshly appearance (2 Corinthians 5:17). God Himself warned mankind not to make any pictures of Him. He called it a corrupt act to do so. His words are: "Lest you act corruptly". The question is, lest you act corruptly in what? "Lest you act" **corrupt** by making false images or false similitude of God according to corrupt mankind (Romans 1:23). Remember, the children of Israel did not see any bodily representation of God in Mount Horeb. God did not want them to corrupt the image of Him. There is only one true image of God, Jesus — the Lamb of God (Colossians 1:15; Hebrews 1:2-4). Other images of Jesus made by man are always corruptible.

Romans 1:23, NKJV: And **changed** *the glory of the incorruptible God into an* **image** *made like* **corruptible man** *— and birds and four-footed animals and creeping things*

Any image of Jesus, made by man, is corruptible. The Black Jesus and the White Jesus, these images are corruptible. Why? "He (Jesus) hath no form (lit., representation)" [Isaiah 53:2]. The word **"form"** also means "delineation" (see Strong's Concordance).

"**Delineation**" means the act of representing. None have represented the maimed Lamb bodily; neither will any represent Him. To God, man's image of Jesus is corruptible (Romans 1:23). This generation did not see Him; therefore, we do not have the right to make any corrupt icons.

Deuteronomy teaches that humanity will corrupt God's image, and themselves, especially, when they make Him to look like any similitude of "male" and "female" (Deuteronomy 4:16). Two reasons for this are: 1). Only God knew how Jesus would look when He came to the earth; and 2). after Adam and Eve sinned, they birthed children after their image, not God's image (Genesis 5:3).

The image of man (Adam's) is opposite the image of God (Christ). One must remember God is irregular compared to man. For example, God's day **begins** in the **evening** and **ends** in the **morning** (Genesis 1). A good way of looking at this truth is that when some want to sleep, God wants to talk. God is opposite man.

God's truth concerning Jesus is also opposite man's doctrine today. Today, man teaches that Jesus is handsome relative to their standard, but God is opposite this. The proof is He made our Lord the most disfigured man who ever lived or will live (Isaiah 52:14).

There is no form (representation or outline) for Jesus. God made Him disfigured, thus it is difficult to copy His image. It was also difficult for people to look at His face. Jesus was so ugly man despised Him and hid their faces from Him.

It took someone hungry for God's true beauty to look past Jesus' physical ugliness. **This shows the truth that one must be able to see inner beauty in all of God's creation.** Even though Jesus was disfigured bodily, the beauty of **God's express image (lit.,**

character; Hebrews1:3), radiated from Him. The inward character of the Lamb of God was so beautiful people that flocked to Him.

All who believed in the Lord, when He walked the earth as a man, had to look past His disfigurement. However, there were many who were stunned at his "marred" (disfigured) "visage" (or beauty). Yet, the beauty of this was that, through this ugliness, He was able to sprinkle many (Luke 7:36-47; Isaiah 54:15).

The Scripture (Isaiah 52:14) first describes Jesus' ugliness. Then it says, **"So shall he sprinkle many nations" (Isaiah 54:15).** One might ask, "How does the Lamb's ugliness sprinkle many nations?"

An interpretation is this: because of His ugliness, He is able to **"sprinkle,"** that is, heal with His **blood.** He is able to heal those who feel they are ugly. Thus, comfort comes to those who allow Him to heal them by his blood.

Another way Jesus heals those with self-esteem problems is: He can inform the believer as to why He created body parts. For example, the Lord made the **nose to breathe** (in God's breath Genesis 2:7). He made the **eyes to see** (God) Matthew 5:8, Revelation 1:12). **The hair is for covering,** or protection (II Kings 1:8, Matthew 3:4). Finally, the **mouth was created to speak** (praises to God, etc., Psalm 149:6), and **the ear to hear** (Revelation 2:29).

Therefore, do not despise your looks, or anyone else's. One should not even feel deprived relative to someone else. If one despises his, or her looks, they are actually despising the image of God (Genesis 1:27). If anyone feels he/she is not beautiful according to today's standard, remember God makes nothing ugly. "He hath made **everything beautiful** in his time" (Ecclesiastes 3:11).

Yet, if one is handsome or beautiful, he/she should not feel bad, because of this teaching. Esther, Daniel, Mishael, Hananiah and Azariah were good looking (Esther 2:7, Daniel 1:4). David was handsome (I Samuel 16:12), and God used him mightily.

Joseph and his mother were good-looking (Genesis 39:6; 29:17), yet God guided him to rulership. But note, even though David and Joseph were handsome, it was their heart (inward beauty) that attracted God to them (I Samuel 16: 7-12, Genesis 39:1-13).

The point is this: whether one is ugly or good-looking according to today's standards, "He (God) hath **made everything beautiful in his time..." (Ecclesiastes 3:11).** To God, everyone who is born in the earth is beautiful.

All are created in His image, and God is not ugly according to man's standards. We are **"fearfully and wonderfully made"** by God (Psalm 139:14). In other words, when God made you, He was too **fearful** to make a mistake. Thus, however you look; it is **wonderfully** beautiful to God.

BEAUTY

There are many Hebrew words translated to mean beauty. One of them is **Yophiy (yof-ee).** The root for Yophiy is **Yophah (yaw-faw),** which means **to be bright.** Therefore, **beauty is brightness,** and brightness has to do with character (compare Hebrews 1:3). Thus, beauty is **within.**

*Psalms 45:11, KJV: So, shall the **king** greatly desire thy **beauty (root: brightness)** for he is the Lord, and worship thou him.*

*Psalms 45:13, KJV: The **king's** daughter is all glorious **within:** her clothing [within] is of wrought gold.*

The "king" in verse eleven is the Lord. He greatly desires everyone's beauty (brightness). In other words, God wants to see His brightness in you as you "worship" him. In the words of Psalm 45:13, "The king's daughter is **all glorious within**" (Compare Songs of Solomon 2:14). His (God's) "daughter" (symbolic of the Church) is all glorious **within.** God sees true beauty as brightness, **within.**

This goes for all in the earth who have the brightness of God shining through their hearts (2 Peter 1:19). Therefore, regardless of what a person feels about his/her appearance, God considers that person beautiful when Brightness (Jesus') is on the inside (compare Matthew 6:22-23). **Therefore, ugliness is the opposite of brightness.** The opposite of brightness is darkness.

This darkness is on the inside of peoples' heart, not outward appearance. There are many beautiful people outwardly; yet they are ugly on the inside. With this in mind, one can easily understand **"what"** makes one ugly.

The **"what"** is the ugliness of sin! This is why we, the believers, must preach the Gospel. Sin, which causes ugliness, can only be healed by Him who can identify with ugliness to its fullest. The Church must be **timely** in presenting Jesus to this generation. Why? Beauty also has to do with **timing.** Remember, "He hath made everything beautiful in **his time...." (Ecclesiastes3: 11, KJV).**

One of the Greek words translated to mean "beautiful" is **horaious,** which comes from the word **hora ("hour")** [Romans 10:15]. **"Horaious"** means belonging to the right hour or season **(timely)** [Strong's # 5611]. This compliments the verse from the book of Ecclesiastes 3:11, partially stated above. Let us see how it is used in the book of Romans.

*Romans 10:15, NKJV: And how shall they preach unless they are sent? As it is written: "How **beautiful (lit., timely)** are the feet of those who preach the gospel of peace, who bring glad tidings of good things!"*

In this verse, we see beauty is preaching the Gospel (the good news). It is the beautiful (timely) message of the Gospel of Jesus that God sees as good. For example, the timely message of this book is helping the reader even now. How? The reader is hearing "glad tiding of good things!"

The **"good thing"** that Jesus can identify with one's ugliness is helping in the area of self-esteem. Thus, one becomes "glad" (happy) to hear such good news. Can you see it now? "He hath made everything **beautiful in his time**" (Ecclesiastes 3:11).

Yet, ironically, it is for this very beauty (brightness of the Gospel; 2 Corinthians 4:4) our Lord was killed. "Who being **the brightness of His glory and the express image (lit., character) of His [God's] person ...**" (Hebrews 1:3). Men despised His outward ugliness; and they also hated His light (the brightness of the beauty of His internal character).

They hated His internal beauty because, to the persecutors, the Lamb's internal beauty did not match their expectation of God's behavior towards the sinners and depraved.

His beautiful news (gospel) that the poor can also have the King's domain working in their lives was not liked by the religious folks. His beautiful news that the tax collectors (the rich) can also be forgiven was not liked by the "orthodox" of His day.

Whenever the Lamb demonstrated beauty by comforting the depraved (poor depraved or the rich depraved) He was assassinated with words. This was the same treatment that was dished out to those who did not have the "beauty" according to the religious standard of that age.

Yet, in all the ugly appearances of the Lamb, He was able to comfort His followers out of His internal beauty. He knew He was from God regardless of what He looked like on the outside. Jesus is from God just as you and I are, no matter our appearances. It is the internal beauty that matters. He was made worthy to heal us because of His love for His beautiful creation.

The **slain Lamb** is **worthy** to heal all who feel slain for their ugliness. The **ugly Lamb** can **comfort us** in all our pains. The Lamb of God restored positive self-concepts to His creation in spite of what our circumstances may look like on the outside.

He is our beauty in any appearance problem we may feel ashamed of. He is our comfort in any appearance problem we may face with our own faces. Jesus is the High Priest who comforts us in all our pressures of life that may appear contrary to the standards of this age. He overcame similar circumstances.

UGLY CIRCUMSTANCES – PRIESTLY COMFORT

*Hebrews 4:14, NKJV: For we do not have a High Priest who cannot **sympathize** with our **weaknesses**, but was in all points tempted as we are, yet without sin.*

*Matthew 8:19-21, N KJV: ¹⁹Then a certain scribe came and said to Him, "Teacher, I will follow You wherever You go." ²⁰And Jesus said to him, "Foxes have holes and birds of the air have nests, **but the Son of Man has nowhere to lay His head."***

*1 Corinthians 4:9-11, NKJV: ... **We have been made a spectacle to the world, both to angels and to men** ... and **we are poorly clothed**, and beaten, and **homeless**.*

John 1:45-46, NKJV: ⁴⁵*Philip found Nathanael and said to him, "We have found ... Jesus **of Nazareth**, the son of Joseph."* ⁴⁶*And Nathanael said to him, "**Can anything good come out of Nazareth?**"*

*2 Kings 2:23, NKJV: Then he [Elisha] went up from there to Bethel; and as he was going up the road, some youths came from the city and mocked him, and said to him, "**Go up, you baldhead! Go up, you baldhead!**"*

From the Scriptures above, we can see above some of the ugly circumstances of life. You have Jesus who did not have a place to lay His Head. There is Paul (a sent apostle) and other Believers who were poorly clothed, homeless, and spectacles because of their circumstances. Jesus was raised in a bad city—Baltimore, Maryland, "oops," I mean Nazareth. Elisha was teased for his baldheadedness. This sounds like most of us, doesn't it? Those who are critical always see the outward bad and not the inward good.

You may have been brought up in an ugly city—the ghetto. This does not change the beauty that the Lord has placed **in** you. You can rise from that and move to a "heavenly city." You may be scantily clothed on the outside yet clothed with glory and honor "within." You may not currently have a certain dwelling place; yet there is a place in Jesus. Your hair may be falling out like Elisha. He (the Lord Jesus) can give you hair.

I remember in the early 1990's a Sister came to me with her daughter's hair falling out; I mean she had nothing but patches of short hair. I laid my hand on her daughter's hair and prayed for it. The next time I saw the little girl, her hair had grown down to the middle of her back. The Lamb can comfort you because He felt what all humanity feels deep on the inside. He gives beauty for ashes. He is our Sympathizer.

This is true for any other area of our lives. Jesus has been tempted in every way. Jesus was made a spectacle for our healing. This includes being judged for ugliness relative to the beauty of the beast system. How does the Lord heal us? He does it by teaching us to love ourselves no matter what we or our circumstances look like. The Scripture teaches us to love our neighbor **as ourselves** (Luke 10:27); with the understanding that the greater love is to love as Jesus, where one lays down his/her life for another, or Jesus preferring the life of another (us) over Himself (1 John 3:16).

With that's said, sometimes a person can only treat (love) his/her neighbors the way he/she feels about his/herself. Another way of saying this is, the degree of "love" one has for himself/herself is the degree of love one can show to his/her neighbor. In other words, people treat other people the way they feel about themselves. So, people must love as God loves and also love themselves as God loves them, that is, prefer others over yourself and accept how Jesus created you and them through God's eternal view of us. Then, they can love their neighbors properly, even those neighbors who look down on people who do not look like them. This is accomplished as one realizes that Jesus was also tempted in this manner; yet He loved others when they did not love themselves.

Thus, Jesus can heal all who feel ugly according to this world's standard. Jesus knew that He was not ugly. He knew that God "fearfully and wonderfully" made him. He knew He possessed the beauty of God. Jesus knew Who He had on the inside—the Father of spirits, the Father of lights.

Remember the Lord loves you for who you are on the inside. **He forever stands as a High Priest to sympathize—have a fellow feeling—with us.** Now, I am not referring to our Lord having pity party with our low thinking. What I am referring to is His confidence being discovered in us.

When one of the lame that He healed was having a pity party concerning his circumstances, Jesus did not get commiserate with the man's ugly circumstance. He confidently asked the man, "Do you want to be made well?" Jesus then confidently said, "Rise ..." (John 5:1-9). I, therefore, pray that each of you, reading this, will allow the grace of our Lord Jesus to heal you completely. May you be confident in who you are on the inside through Him who is "within." Do this and your confidence (beauty) of the Lord within will eventually show on the outside.

THE LAMB'S EYES

*Revelation 5:6, NKJV: And I looked, and behold, in the midst of the throne and of the four living creatures, and in the midst of the elders, stood a Lamb as though it had been slain, having seven horns and **seven eyes**, which are **the seven Spirits of God** sent out into all the earth.*

The Lamb has "seven eyes, which are the seven Spirits of God." One of the meanings of the seven eyes is that the Lamb, and those with the Lamb's nature, see all things (1 John 2:20). One of the most lacking areas in the Church of Jesus is the ability to see or discern.

The ability is available; however, some do not make use of it. God has placed in our hearts the Lamb of God with His seven eyes. The seven eyes are the "seven Spirits of God." Thus, the Lamb's eyes are linked to the Holy Spirit. However, before I develop the seven eyes of the Holy Spirit, let us first discover what the seven Spirits of God are.

*Isaiah 11:1-2, NKJV: [1]There shall come forth a Rod from the stem of Jesse, and a Branch shall grow out of his roots. [2]The Spirit of the **LORD** shall rest upon Him, the Spirit of **wisdom** and **understanding,** the Spirit of **counsel** and **might,** the Spirit of **knowledge** and of the **fear of the LORD.***

There is "The Spirit of the Lord," "The Spirit of Wisdom," The Spirit of ... Understanding," "The Spirit of Counsel," "The Spirit of ...Might," "The Spirit of Knowledge," and "The Spirit ... of the fear of the Lord." These total seven to me.

These seven Spirits of God are called eyes because "the Lord" is an "eye" of God (2 Chronicles 11:9); thus, "wisdom" is an "eye;" "counsel" is an "eye;" "understanding" is an "eye;" and so on. What is the purpose for eyes? Eyes were created to see.

THOUGHTS CAN BE SEEN

*Matthew 9:4, NKJV: But **Jesus, knowing (lit., seeing) their thoughts**, said, "Why do you think evil in your hearts?*

"Knowing" in the verse above is the Greek word **"edio"** which properly means, to **"see,"** by implication, **"to know."** Thus, the word means **"to know by seeing."** Jesus demonstrated His spiritual sight. The Lamb of God could see "thoughts." Thus, He could address certain thoughts of action that were leveled against Him. This ability to see is a function of the Holy Spirit that has to be manifested through the Church.

The Lamb of God was able to address certain issues with people by the ability to see thoughts. Jesus answered the religious folks according to the thoughts of their hearts, not according to their disguised words. The Church must get out of her state of ignorance by allowing the seven eyes of the Lamb to see through her. A Christian can see thoughts and motives. Paul indicated that the ability of the seven eyes relative to seeing thoughts is also operational in "us."

*2 Corinthians 2:11, NKJV: Lest Satan should take advantage of **us**; for **we** are not ignorant of his **devices (lit., thoughts)**.*

*2 Corinthians 10:4-5, NKJV: 4For the weapons of our warfare are not carnal but mighty in God for pulling down strongholds, 5casting down arguments and every high thing that exalts itself against the knowledge of God, bringing every **thought (Gk., noema)** into captivity to the obedience of Christ*

*2 Corinthians 3:14, NKJV: But their **minds (or thoughts)** were blinded. For until this day the same veil remains unlifted in the reading of the Old Testament, because the veil is taken away in Christ.*

The words "devices," "thoughts" and "minds" highlighted in the verses above are all the same Greek word—noema—which means perception, intellect, mind, thought, etc. (see Strong's Concordance). Therefore, Paul was saying "we are not ignorant of [the tempter's] **thoughts."**

Now do not get spooked out by going around listening for Satan's thought. That is not the intent here! The intent is to be able to recognize (discern) the enemy's thoughts, to be able to bring "every thought into captivity to the obedience of Christ." This should not be strange to you. The Lamb of God also exposed the thoughts of the tempter.

Matthew 16:21-23, NKJV: [21]*From that time Jesus began to show to His disciples that He must go to Jerusalem and suffer many things from the elders and chief priests and scribes, and be killed, and be raised the third day.* [22]*Then Peter took Him aside and began to rebuke Him, saying, "Far be it from You, Lord; this shall not happen to You!"* [23]*But He turned and said to Peter,* **"Get behind Me, Satan!** *You are an offense to Me, for you are not* **mindful** *of the things of God, but the things of men."*

The Lord's mind was to suffer at Jerusalem. Peter, at that time, thought that Jesus was out of His mind. The Lord aptly corrected Peter by telling Peter that he was out of the Lord's mind and walking in the mind of another. The Lord called Peter "Satan;" and indicated to "Satan" that he was not **"mindful"** of the things of God. The Lord demolished the stronghold of the tempter's thoughts by addressing the "mind." Jesus, the Word of God, sees every thought.

THE WORD HAS EYES

Hebrews 4:12-13, NKJV: [12]*For* **the word of God** *... is a discerner of the* **thoughts** *and intents of the heart.* [13]*And there is no creature hidden* *from His sight, but all things are naked and open to the **eyes** of Him to whom we must give account.*

The Word of God is a discerner of thoughts. The writer of Hebrews also calls the Word of God, "the eyes of Him to whom we must give account." Therefore, our thoughts are accountable to God. Yet, there is more!

If, the Word of God has the ability to discern thought, and it does, then if the Church put the Word of God in her heart, guess what the Church becomes? The Church will have the same abilities as the Word of God—"all things are ...open to [His] eyes..." Who is in her!

Thus, the seven eyes of the Lamb of God also work through the Word of God. The Word of God is a **"discerner"** which is transliterated as "critical" from the Greek word **"kritikós."** The seven eyes of the Spirit are balanced by the "critical" eyes of the Word of God. In other words, the written Word tempers any excessive discernment. In addition, the point still stands; the Word of God sees thoughts and motives.

During the early 1990s, while I was renovating a building where a Church met, the pastor came out of his office after counseling someone. I remember vividly hearing his thoughts saying, "I wonder if I counseled her correctly?" I relayed to him what I heard his mind say and encouraged him that God had indeed heard his concerns. The Lamb of God uses His seven eyes of the Spirit to see and search the **minds** and **hearts**.

EYES LIKE A FLAME

Revelation 2:18-23, NKJV: [18]*"And to the angel of the church in Thyatira write, 'These things says the Son of God, who has **eyes like a flame of*** *fire...* ²³*... I am He who **searches the minds and hearts**. And I will give to each one of you according to your works ...."*

Have you ever noticed that when parents are present with their children, the child's behavior is usually more becoming? The same is true for the Church of Jesus. His flaming eyes are reminders of His ability to "search **minds (lit., kidneys, figuratively the inmost mind)** and hearts" of those in the Church.

His Paternal care is present through His watchful eyes. However, His watchful eyes are not always to point out the negative. The eyes of the Lamb are also as dove's eyes, and He looks for that which is positive. Paul used this ability of the Spirit in his epistles.

*Colossians 2:4-6, NKJV: For though **I am absent in the flesh, yet I am with you in spirit**, rejoicing to see your good order and the steadfastness of your faith in Christ.*

Paul was absent in the flesh; or he was not there physically. Yet Paul was **"with [them] in spirit."** The eyes of the Spirit is ever present, rejoicing to see our **"good order"** — the Melchizedek **order** — and our "steadfast... faith in Christ." The Lambs seven eyes are like flames. They penetrate all things. His eyes transcend **distance**.

John 1:47-48, NKJV: ⁴⁷*Jesus saw Nathanael coming toward Him, and said of him, "Behold, an Israelite indeed, in whom is no deceit!"* ⁴⁸*Nathanael said to Him, "How do You know me?" Jesus answered and said to him, "Before Philip called you, when you were under the fig tree, I **saw** you."*

Jesus saw Nathanael under the fig tree **before** Nathanael met Jesus in person. Whatever Nathanael was doing under the fig tree, he was not using "trickery" — which is the meaning of "deceit" in this Scripture. The seven eyes of the Spirit were at work in Jesus; and

He spoke an encouraging word to Nathanael. The lamb's eyes, ability to see, brought about an interesting result.

Nathanael, declared Jesus to be "the Son of God" and the "King of Israel." The eyes of the Lord will cause belief in the Son-ship and Kingship of the Lamb of God. The Lamb Himself said, "Because I said to you, 'I **saw** you under the fig tree,' do you **believe**? You will see greater things than these" (John 1:50). The Lord's eyes are "strong" towards those whose hearts are "loyal" to Him. Yes! His eyes penetrate. Yes! His eyes are like flames. Yet, they are as "harmless as doves." He is pure in the way He sees. The Lamb has dove's eyes.

DOVE'S EYES

*Matthew 10:16, NKJV: Behold, I send you out as sheep in the midst of wolves. Therefore, be wise as serpents and **harmless as doves.***

*Song of Solomon 5:12, NKJV: **His eyes are like doves** by the rivers of waters, washed with milk, and fitly set.*

*Luke 3:21-22, NKJV: 21When all the people were baptized, it came to pass that Jesus also was baptized; and while He prayed, the heaven was opened. 22And the **Holy Spirit** descended in **bodily form like a dove upon Him**, and a voice came from heaven which said, "You are My beloved Son; in You I am well pleased."*

"Harmless," as referenced above, literally means to be **"unmixed"** according to Strong's Concordance. In the love Song between Solomon, (who is symbolic of the Lamb) and the Shulamite (symbolic of the Lamb's Wife), she indicated that her Lover (Jesus) had "eyes like doves." According to Luke 3:22, the **Spirit** has a "**bodily** form like a dove." Thus, the seven Spirits of God have seven eyes like doves.

Doves, according to Jesus, see in an **"unmixed"** fashion. The eyes of the Lamb are pure. The Church of Jesus must see in the same way. We must see purely. We should not see in mixture. This means the Church is not to be corrupted by "mystery Babylon" — the harlot — and the mother of harlots. Peter indicated that there will be some whose eyes will be filled of the adulteress (Babylon); therefore, they will not see with purity.

2 Peter 2:12-14, NKJV: ¹²*But these, like natural brute beasts ..., * ¹⁴***having eyes full of adultery (lit., adulteress)*** *and that cannot cease from sin ...*

Revelation 17:1-5, NKJV: Then one of the seven angels who had the seven bowls came and talked with me, saying to me, "Come, I will show you the judgment of **the great harlot** *...* **MYSTERY, BABYLON** *THE GREAT, THE MOTHER OF HARLOTS AND OF THE ABOMINATIONS OF THE EARTH.*

This is the adulteress that the Holy Spirit through Peter was referring to. Those who are possessed by her do not see unmixed. The Hebrew definition for Babylon is **"mixture."** The Greek definition of Babylon is **"confusion."** Thus, those whose eyes are full of the adulteress, see through confusion and mixture. The Lamb's eyes are different.

His eyes are "dove's eyes." The Lamb of God sees everything purely. The Church must allow this unmixed sight of the Lamb to see through her. Adulterous eyes cause one not to discern purely. Doves eyes — eyes of the seven Spirits — cause the Church to see people in an unmixed manner. In fact, the Shulamite (the Church) eventually receives an impartation of the dove's eyes from her Lover.

*Song of Solomon 1:15, NKJV: Behold ...***You have dove's eyes.**

She became "one" with her husband. She began to see as He sees. The Church must see with the same eyes as her Husband. The eyes of the dove see in people what they can become in the Lord. The dove's eyes are not judgmental to the point of hurting people by condemning them for their sins or faults. This is difficult sometimes; especially with those who may have adversely hurt you.

However, even on the cross, Jesus forgave the very ones who crucified Him (Luke 23:34). He saw that they could still, potentially, be saved. We must always see as a dove to exemplify the light of forgiveness.

SEVEN TORCHES

Revelation 4:5, NKJV: And from the throne proceeded lightnings, thunderings, and voices. **Seven lamps (lit., torches) of fire** *were burning before the throne,* **which are the seven Spirits of God.**

The **seven** Spirits of God are His "finished ("7") work" being implemented by the Holy Spirit—"And on the **seventh** day God **ended (lit., to be finished)** His work..." (Genesis 2:2). On the cross the Lamb of God said, **"It is finished!"** The seven Spirits are sent into all the earth to bring those who accept Jesus to the finished (restful) place in Him—"Jesus, the author and **finisher** of our faith ..." (Hebrews 12:2, NKJV).

The **seven** torches are His complete light which allows His Church to see properly. Torches are used for light. One of the purposes for light is for sight in a dark place. In Zechariah, the **lampstand** has **"seven lamps."** The lampstand has the light of the seven lamps defined as the "eyes of the Lord which scan ... the whole earth."

Zechariah 4:1-10, NKJV: ¹*Now the angel who talked with me came back and wakened me, as a man who is wakened out of his sleep.* ²*and he said* to me, "What do you see?"   So, I said, "I am looking, and there is a **lampstand** of solid gold with a bowl on top of it, and on the stand **seven lamps** with seven pipes to the seven lamps. ... ⁴So I answered and spoke to the angel who talked with me, saying, "What are these, my lord?" ⁵Then the angel who talked with me answered and said to me ...**They are the eyes of the LORD,** Which scan to and fro throughout the whole earth."

2 Chronicles 16:9, NKJV: *For the **eyes of the LORD** run to and fro throughout the whole earth, to show Himself strong on behalf of those whose heart is **loyal (lit., complete)** to Him.*

The lampstand is a symbol the Lamb's Church (Revelation 1:20). The seven lampstands are also the seven eyes of the Lord going here and there in the earth, through His Church. The lampstand(s) are lit by the light of the seven Torches (Spirits) of God. In the tabernacle of Moses, the lampstand was filled with oil for light. Oil is symbolic of the Holy Spirit.

1 Samuel 16:1, NKJV: *Now the LORD said to Samuel, "How long will you mourn for Saul, seeing I have rejected him from reigning over Israel? **Fill your horn with oil** and go; I am sending you to Jesse the Bethlehemite. For I have provided Myself a king among his sons."*

1 Samuel16:13, NKJV: *Then Samuel took the horn of oil and **anointed** him in the midst of his brothers; and the **Spirit of the LORD** came upon David from that day forward. So, Samuel arose and went to Ramah.*

 Therefore, the seven Spirits, through His omnipresence, are the Oil in the lampstand (the Church). He is also the "lamps" (torches) on the seven lampstands that provide light for sight. In the words of Zechariah, the **"lampstand**…and …the seven **lamps**…are the eyes of the Lord." This should not be strange to you because the Lamb's nature is called light. In reference to New Jerusalem, "The Lamb is its Light" (Revelation 21:23, last part)

LIGHT TO SEE

*John 12:35, NKJV: Then Jesus said to them, "A little while longer the light is with you. Walk while you have the **light**, lest darkness overtake you; he who walks in darkness does not **know (lit., see)** where he is going.*

Revelation 21:23 (last part), NKJV: ...The Lamb is the Light.

We need the seven torches of the Spirit to "see where [we are] going." The Lamb of God (His character) is **the Light** that causes one to see. The more we take on the character of the Lamb, the more light we manifest. The easier it is to **see**. In other words, the seven eyes of the Lamb also function as the seven torches when we walk in the Lamb's nature.

Again, the purpose of the torches is for sight. Some, in the Church and outside the Church, cannot see. They need the fire of the Spirit to enlighten their eyes. Thus, Jesus' "eyes like a flame of **fire**" (Revelation 1:114) are linked to "the seven torches of **fire**" (Revelation 4:5). Saying it another way, the Lamb's eyes (His ability to see) bring to light (via the seven lamps of fire) His death, burial, and resurrection into the hearts of His creation.

APOSTOLIC EYES

*Revelation 5:6, NKJV: And I looked, and behold, in the midst of the throne and of the four living creatures, and in the midst of the elders, stood a Lamb as though it had been slain, having seven horns and **seven eyes**, which are the seven Spirits of God **sent** out into all the earth.*

The Greek word used for "sent" in the verse above is "apostello," and according to Vine's Expository Dictionary, this word is "<u>akin</u> to "apostolos" — apostles. There are manifestations (plural) of apostles. The seven eyes are "apostello" (sent) through His apostles in their various manifestations. Jesus indicated that John the Baptist was "more than a prophet" (Matthew 11:9). Scholars have debated what this means. However, the answer is simple.

Matthew 11:9-10, NKJV: ⁹*But what did you go out to see? A prophet? Yes, I say to you, and* **more than a prophet.** ¹⁰*For this is he of whom it is written: 'Behold, I* **send (apostello)** *My messenger before Your face, who will prepare Your way before You.'*

Jesus was the one who made the statement that John the Baptist was "more than a prophet." Therefore, the Lamb of God also had the answer. The answer is found in the rest of Jesus' statement. "For this is he whom …I send [apostello]…." John the Baptist was more than a prophet because he was an "apostolic prophet." Peter was more than an apostle; he was a pastoral apostle (Luke 6:13-14 w/John 21:16).

John, the beloved was more than an apostle; he was a prophetic apostle (Luke 6:13-14, Revelation 10:11; 22:9, etc.), Paul was more than an apostle. He was a teaching, evangelistic and prophetic apostle (1 Timothy 2:7 w/ Acts 13:1).

The purpose of this understanding is not to stress title, as some are doing today. The purpose of this understanding is to stress "function." It is also worthy to note that becoming a mature "son" is "more excellent" than being called a bishop, and so on.

With the above statements in mind, one can see that the seven horns and the seven eyes are manifested through apostles — pastoral apostles, prophetic apostles, teaching apostles, evangelistic apostles. These are apostles with a measure of the other four gifts. Or there are apostolic pastors, apostolic prophets, and so on (these are pastors, teachers, and the like who have an apostolic measure).

The latter are not apostles in the strictest sense of the word. Yet they manifest a measure of the apostolic nature. They "function" in the seven apostolic Spirits.

This is why there seems to be an abundance of foundational judgments being manifest by various leaders. However, in continuing on, apostles have the ability to see (via the seven Spirits) things that is not readily apparent; and they deal with sight. (A note in passing: one qualification for an apostle is that they usually have **seen** the Lord (1 Corinthians 9:1).

*Acts 13:9-12, NKJV: ⁹Then Saul, who also is called Paul, **filled** with the **Holy Spirit, looked intently** at him ¹⁰and said, "O full of all deceit and all fraud, you son of the devil, you enemy of all righteousness, will you not cease perverting the straight ways of the Lord? ¹¹And now, indeed, the hand of the Lord is upon you, and you shall be blind, **not seeing** the sun for a time." And immediately a dark mist fell on him, and he went around seeking someone to lead him by the hand. ¹²Then the proconsul **believed**, when he saw what had been done, being astonished at the teaching of the Lord.*

Paul through the "Holy Spirit"—the seven Spirits of the Lamb of God—**"looked intently"** via the seven eyes of the Lamb of God. He saw the heart and motives of the sorcerer. Apostles or apostolic prophets do see (2 Corinthians 12:1-4; Acts 14:9; 2 Kings 5:26; Revelation 1:12, etc.).

In the verses above, Paul saw what this false prophet was really about. The false prophet was "…perverting the straight (or immediate[3]) ways of the Lord…." The result was judgment on the

---

[3] Sometimes when things do not happen "immediately" on our behalf, one of the reasons could be the presence of Jannes and Jambres types (2 Timothy 2:8; Acts 13:8 w/13:10; Exodus 7:22).

eyes of this false one—"… [The false prophet] shall be **blind, not seeing** the sun for a time." The Lamb of God is allowing the manifestation of His seven eyes through His apostles and His blood bought Church.

This is the season when the Church will become "more than" children being tossed and carried about by every false doctrine (see Ephesians 4:14). She will be matured into the five measures of the grace gifts, especially the apostolic measure. She will be "apostello"—sent—by the seven eyes to bring deliverance to the groaning creation. The Church will finally have the mature mind of the Lamb of God to see like the Man Himself (John 4:16-19 w/John 4:29 and 1 Corinthians 13:11).

THE LAMB'S HEAD

Exodus 12:5-9, NKJV: *⁵**Your lamb** shall be without blemish, a male of the first year. You may take it from the sheep or from the goats.... ⁹Do not eat it raw, nor boiled at all with water, but roasted in fire – **its head with its legs and its entrails.***

During the Feast of Passover, the Israelites were required to eat the head, legs, and entrails of the lamb. The head holds the brains of the Lamb. Thus, there is a requirement to eat the brain of the true Lamb—Jesus, the Christ. The head with its brain is an example of us consuming the mind of Christ. We do not have to eat the literal flesh of His head today. However, we are required to eat the brain of His head **in Spirit**.

John 6:51-63, NKJV: *⁵¹I am the living bread which came down from heaven. If anyone eats of this bread, he will live forever; and **the bread that I shall give is My flesh**, which I shall give for the life of the world." ⁵²**The Jews therefore quarreled among themselves, saying, "How can this Man give us His flesh to eat?"** ⁵³Then Jesus said to them, "**Most assuredly, I say to you, unless you eat the flesh of the Son of Man and drink His blood, you have no life in you** .... ⁶¹When Jesus knew in Himself that His disciples complained about this, He said to them, "Does this offend you? ⁶² What then if you should see the Son of Man ascend where He was before? ⁶³It is the Spirit who gives life; the flesh profits nothing. **The words that I speak to you are spirit**, and they are life.*

We must interpret the Old Testament in light of the New Testament. Jesus' flesh and Jesus' blood are spiritual according to the Lamb Himself. Jesus said this before He was crucified.

"Unless you eat the flesh of the Son of Man and drink His blood, you have no life in you... the flesh profits nothing. The words

that I speak to you are spirit...." The same is true for the quote from Exodus concerning eating the head of the lamb—"the flesh [brain] profits nothing. The words ... are spirit."

The Lord is not looking for us to eat the head of a literal sacrifice. The Lamb of God is the sacrifice. He died once. He was sacrificed once. We do not have any right to institute animal sacrifice again. He abolished animal sacrifice almost 2,000 years ago. We eat His head through the Spirit. The head that we eat today is His spiritual mind. As indicated earlier, it is not the literal brain of a Lamb.

In the mid-1990s, while I was in college, I was talking with a group. One of the persons happened to be African (we were reviewing some formulas and ended up discussing the fact that homoerotic acts are abuse of the male body). After the discussion, as we were going our several ways, the young man from Africa replied to me by saying, **"Donald! I can have your brain, but not your mind."** His reply startled me; and I asked him to explain.

He replied with the same statement. Finally, I gave it some thought. He was saying he had the "brains" to understand our discussion; however, he did not have the "mind" to change his lifestyle to follow Jesus. He distinguished the difference between using the "brain" to understand and having the "mind" to live righteously. My point again, the Lamb's head is not his literal brains. The Lamb's head is the Mind of Christ in Spirit. Yet, how do we eat Spirit? The answer is within Jesus' statement.

The "words" He "speaks," they are "spirit." In other words, as you hear Jesus "speak" to you through his Word and His Holy Spirit, you are actually eating His Head. As the belly digests food, so the spirit of a man digests the Lord.

1 Corinthians 6:13-17, NKJV: **¹³Foods for the stomach and the stomach for foods....** *Now the body is ... for the Lord, and* **the Lord for the body...** **¹⁷***But he who is joined to the* **Lord is one spirit with Him.**

The stomach breaks down food and sends nourishment for the body throughout the body. The body uses the Lord, being one in spirit with Him, to nourish itself spiritually.

When the Lord speaks words of Spirit to you, your body uses (eats) it for nourishment, just like the stomach uses food. When we eat His mind (head) we receive His mind. In fact, the mind of Christ has to do with our **foreheads** being engraved with His name by the ink of the Holy Spirit. The foreheads of the one hundred and forty-four thousand were engraved with the name of God and the name of the Lamb.

THE ONE HUNDRED AND FORTY-FOUR THOUSAND

Revelation 14:1-2, NKJV: Then I looked, and behold, **a Lamb standing** *on Mount Zion, and with Him* **one hundred and forty-four thousand,** *having*[4] *His Father's name* **written on their foreheads.**

Revelation 14:1, NIV: Then I looked, and there before me was **the Lamb,** *standing on Mount Zion, and* **with him 144,000 who had his name and** *his Father's name* **written on their foreheads.**

Revelation 14:1, NASU: Then I looked, and behold, **the Lamb** *was standing on Mount Zion, and with Him* **one hundred and forty-four thousand,** *having* **His name** *and the name of His Father* **written on their foreheads.**

---

[4] The oldest Greek texts included "*His Name and ....*"

*Revelation 14:1, TLB: Then I saw **a Lamb** standing on Mount Zion in Jerusalem, and with him were **144,000** who had **his Name** and his Father's Name **written on their foreheads.***

*Revelation 14:1, RSV: Then I looked, and lo, on Mount Zion stood **the Lamb**, and with him **a hundred and forty-four thousand** who had **his name** and his Father's name **written on their foreheads.***

Before interpreting the meaning of the One Hundred Forty-four thousand, let us look at the Lamb's name written on their **"foreheads."** "Forehead" is a combination of two Greek words, "meta" (change, with, midst, beyond) and "ops" (eyes, sight).

Therefore, the Lamb's name **"changed"** their **eyes** (the way they see). The Lamb's name is in the **"midst"** of their eyes. The Lamb's name was also **"with"** their eyes. Finally, the Lamb's name was **beyond** their eyes. It makes sense if you think of other words with the prefix "meta," for example **metaphysics.**

Metaphysics means "beyond the physical." It follows that "metaops" means "beyond the eyes." The question then must be asked, what is beyond the eyes of a man or woman? The answer is: their minds. Yes! The forehead is a symbol of the mind. Thus, the 144,000 had the mind of the Lamb; or they had the "nature" of the Lamb in their minds. Name means a name, nature, or cause. The Lamb's name in their forehead is the Lamb's nature in their minds. It is that simple.

That is, they have the mind of Christ—they ate the Lamb's brain. Next, let us look at the 144,000. A friend of mine (Brian Gooch) took a test for the Air force some years ago. He aced the test. The instructor asked him, how he was able to get all the answers?

Brian replied to the instructor, "The answer to every question is within the question." The same is true for a seed. As we have learned, in every seed there is a tree. It follows that the answer to every question concerning the Scripture is within the Scriptures. Is the 144,000 spiritual (figurative) or literal? The answer is: Yes![5]

Revelation 21:17, NKJV: Then he measured its wall: **one hundred and forty-four** *cubits, according to the* **measure of a man,** *that is, of an angel.*

Revelation 20:6, NKJV: Blessed and holy is he who has part in the first resurrection. Over such the second death has no power, but they shall be priests of God and of Christ and shall **reign with Him a thousand years.**

One hundred and forty-four is the **"measure of a man."** This is too simple? Yet, the Word of God is not as complex as some have made it. One hundred and forty-four is the measure of a man. One thousand is the ability to 'reign with Him (Christ)" in resurrection power. Jesus is the Man who rules in resurrection power. This same Man is the Son of God! This same Man is the Lamb of God! His name is Jesus, the Christ, and the Son of the Living God. (I felt good saying that—alleluia!) Jesus **is** Lord!

Ephesians 4:11-14, NKJV: [11]*And He Himself gave some to be apostles, some prophets, some evangelists, and some pastors and teachers,* [12] *for the equipping of the saints for the work of ministry, for the edifying of the body of Christ,* [13]*till we all come to the unity of the faith and of the knowledge of the Son of God, to a perfect* **man,** *to the* **measure** *of the* **stature of the fullness of Christ.**

The "measure of a man" is the measure of the "perfect man"—Jesus, the Christ. The Church's goal is to become **like** the "Son of God... the **measure** of the stature of the fullness of Christ."

---

[5] See one of my other books titled: *The Numbers of God*

Therefore, the 144,000 in Revelation 14:1 are those who reached the measure (144 cubits) of the Lamb's nature and character and they "reign (1000) in (resurrection) life by one Jesus Christ" (see Romans 5:17, Romans 6:4, Acts 4:33, Revelation 20:5-7).

In other words, the 144,000 are mature believers who **rule**[6] in resurrection life becoming as "a perfect **man**, to the **measure** of the **stature of the fullness of Christ."** Part of this measure is lamb-like. That is, they have the mind of Christ's Lamb-like nature. Now relative to the rest of the question, is the 144,000 also literal? The answer is yes! The book stated the number.

LET CHRIST JESUS' MIND BE IN YOU

*Philippians 2:5-8, NKJV: ⁵Let this **mind** be in you, which was also in Christ Jesus, ⁶who, being in the form of God, did not consider it robbery to be equal with God, ⁷but made Himself of no reputation, taking the form of a bondservant, and coming in the likeness of men. ⁸And being found in appearance as a man, He **humbled Himself** and became obedient to the point of death, even the death of the cross.*

The mind of Christ is related to submitting to "the death of the cross." Jesus was "equal with God" before He humbled Himself to be the first and only God to die for His creation. Yes, in His equality, He took the "lower" position and died for us.

"Humble" means to bow down to lower, to lower to the ground, etc. The mind of Christ is to have a mind set to bow down to God's desire. Again, I know this is simplified. Yet, it is that simple to understand. On the other hand, I can see how it is difficult sometimes to take up our cross. However, if the Bible states that

---

[6] One thousand is symbolic of resurrection rule with and through Jesus (Revelation 20:5-6). "One thousand" is also linked with the Holies of Holy.

we can have the Mind of Christ, then we can have the same Mind. The Lord will not tell us to do something we cannot do.

*1 Peter 4:1-2, NKJV: Therefore, since Christ **suffered** for us in the flesh, arm yourselves also with the **same mind**, for he who has suffered in the flesh has ceased from sin.*

Peter heard the same sound from the Spirit of Jesus. Suffering is an avenue by which sin "ceases." Peter indicated that suffering in the flesh is the **"same mind"** as Christ. As Christians we will suffer according to the will of God. It is ungodly to say that Christians will not suffer in this life. It is not right to say that we cannot have the Mind of Christ to endure sufferings at times.

*Acts 14:21-22, NKJV: ²¹And when they had preached the gospel to that city and made many disciples, they returned to Lystra, Iconium, and Antioch, ²²strengthening the souls of the disciples, exhorting them to continue in the faith, and saying, "We **must** through **many tribulations** enter the kingdom of God."*

*2 Timothy 3:12, NKJV: Yes, and all who desire to live godly in Christ Jesus **will suffer** persecution.*

Anyone who teaches that we are not to suffer, does **not** "desire to live godly in Christ;" and they do not have the same mind as Christ. Luke stated that "it is necessary as binding" that "through many tribulations" we "enter the kingdom of God." The Church is to arm herself with the "same mind" as Jesus.

The Lamb of God knew He had to suffer tribulation of the cross, and armed (prepared) His mind to embrace the hardship. This is one of the reasons why in Revelation the 144,000 had the Lamb's name—nature, cause, character—written in their foreheads. To become like the Lamb of God is to have His mind. How do we have this "same mind?"

There are three stages to the mind of Christ. There is "repentance (lit., to change (one's) mind)." There are those who are given to the "mind of the Spirit," through being filled with the Spirit. There is also the "renewing of the spirit of the mind." Saying it another way: there are three seals of God; and the third seal is in the forehead or mind.

All three of these stages are linked to the work of the Holy Spirit. Being sealed in the forehead is the same as saying that the mind of Christ is in the Believer. In other words, the more we devour the Lamb's **head**, the more we **think** like Him.

SEALED IN THEIR FOREHEAD

*Revelation 7:2-3, NKJV: ²Then I saw another angel ascending from the east, **having (lit., holding) the seal** of the living God. And he cried with a loud voice to the four angels to whom it was granted to harm the earth and the sea, ³saying, "Do not harm the earth, the sea, or the trees till we have **sealed** the servants of our God on their **foreheads**."*

*Revelation 9:4, NKJV: They were commanded not to harm the grass of the earth, or any green thing, or any tree, but only those men **who do not** have the seal of God on their foreheads.*

"Having the seal of the living[7] God" is a protection. In Revelation, Chapter 7, the sealed were protected from "winds" of doctrines. In Revelation, Chapter 9, the sealed were protected from the locust-scorpions. Thus, the seal of the Living God is important. This seal is the Holy Spirit imparted by God via the hand of His messengers to the mind of the Believers. Allow me to explain.

---

[7] Note: this is a resurrection statement.

*2 Timothy 1:7, NKJV: For God has not given us a **spirit** of fear, but of power and of love and of **a sound mind.***

Paul statement above is full of a lot of truth. Paul indicated that "God has not given us a spirit of fear." The logical question is: what spirit did God give us? He has given us the "spirit ... of power." He has given us the "spirit ... of love. Yes! He has even given us the **"spirit ... of a sound mind."** There is a spirit of a sound mind. The mind is not sound without the Holy Spirit. Saying it another way: the mind is linked to spirit, not necessarily to the soul. We are to "mind the Spirit," according to the Interlinear Transliterated Bible, Biblesoft (Romans 8:6).

*Ephesians 4:23, NKJV: And be renewed in the **spirit of your mind***

If my exegesis of 1Timothy 1:7 was not convincing, this verse above should be. The spirit is in your mind; or your mind is linked to your spirit. This is important to know relative to the Believer's understanding that he/she is sealed with the Holy Spirit when he/she is filled; except, the seal of the Holy Spirit is in the mind of the Believer.

*Ephesians 1:13, NKJV: In Him you also trusted, after you heard the word of truth, the gospel of your salvation; in whom also, having believed, **you were sealed with the Holy Spirit** of promise.*

First, who sealed them? The Holy Spirit! Second, where were they sealed? According to Paul, they were given the **"Spirit of a sound mind"** (2 Timothy 1:7). They were sealed in their mind. They were given the Spirit of the "same" mind as the Lamb of God. Paul use a phrase like "mind the Spirit" in Romans, Chapter 8, according to the Greek text.

*Romans 8:6, NKJV: For to be carnally minded is death, but to be **spiritually minded** is life and peace.*

*Romans 8:6, Interlinear Transliterated Bible (Biblesoft): Tó gár fróneema teés sarkós thánatos tó dé **fróneema toú Pneúmatos** (Eng., **mind the Spirit**) zooeé kaí eireénee.*

We are to "mind the Spirit;" or we are to have the mind of the Spirit. Having a mind that thinks like the Holy Spirit is having the same mind as the Lamb of God. Being sealed in the forehead is the same as having the mind of Christ. When the Holy Spirit filled our minds, we were sealed in our forehead (Greek: metaops—beyond the eyes) at that time. The Lord gave us the Spirit of a sound mind. Let us look at the progression again:

When we first get saved, we "change (our) minds." This is "repentance" which is different from forgiveness. The next step is for the Holy Spirit to **exchange** our mind with the "saved or delivered mind" of Christ—He installs in us the ability of the mind of Christ. Finally, we progressively walk in the mind of Christ. We activate the mind that was installed in us by the Holy Spirit—in the words of Paul— "be renewed (lit., make fresh or youthful) in the **spirit of your mind.**"

We have to regain our memory, so to speak. Our mind has to become one with Christ's mind. Our thought must become His thoughts. The Greek word "logos" (word) also means **expressed thoughts.** Thus, the Word of God is the thoughts of God. Eat His Word and you will get His thoughts. The seal of God then become obvious on the outside of our forehead.

On our foreheads (the way we think) people should see the name of the Lamb of God written. Ministers use the ink of the Spirit to write on the foreheads of Believers who are in Jesus Christ. The angel in Revelation, Chapter 7 sealed the servants of the living God. These servants are the Israel of God—the Church. Paul picks it up and says we are sealed with the Holy Spirit of Promise. This seal is imparted by the laying on of hands.

SEALED BY THE SPIRIT, THROUGH MAN'S HANDS

*Revelation 7:2-3, NKJV: ²Then I saw another angel ascending from the east, **having (lit., holding) the seal** of the living God…³saying, "Do not harm … till **we** have **sealed** the servants of our God on their **foreheads**."*

For the student of the Word, the angel (singular) is also called a "we." Second, this angel or messengers (plural) were "holding" the seal. The most practical place that the seal could be held is the "hand." The seal is imparted on the forehead by the laying on of hands. The book of Acts exemplified this very clearly.

*Acts 19:1-2, 6, NKJV: ¹And it happened, while Apollos was at Corinth, that Paul, having passed through the upper regions, came to Ephesus. And finding some **disciples** ² he said to them, "Did you receive the Holy Spirit when you believed?" So, they said to him, "We have not so much as heard whether there is a Holy Spirit." …. ⁶And when Paul had **laid hands** on them, **the Holy Spirit** came upon them, and they spoke with tongues and prophesied.*

*Ephesians 1:13, NKJV: In … whom also, having believed, **you were sealed with the Holy Spirit** of promise*

According to Luke above, Paul met some disciples at Ephesus who believed; yet they were not filled (sealed) with the Holy Spirit. These are the same group Paul wrote about in Ephesians 1:13. They were **filled ("sealed")** after Paul **"laid hands** on them." They "were sealed with the Holy Spirit." The Holy Spirit is the seal. Apostles and prophets carry this seal of the living God in their hands.

Apostles and prophets (then and now) "hold" the seal of the living God in their hands. They are the "messengers," [8] the "we," in Revelation, Chapter 7. In other words, we are sealed with the Holy Spirit when the Holy Spirit fills us. This is usually done by the laying on of hands of those who are the holding ones of the Holy Spirit.

Acts 8:14-18, NKJV: **¹⁴***Now when the* **apostles** *who were at Jerusalem heard that Samaria had received the word of God, they sent Peter and John to them,* **¹⁵***who, when they had come down, prayed for them that they might receive the Holy Spirit.* **¹⁶***For as yet He had fallen upon none of them. They had only been baptized in the name of the Lord Jesus.* **¹⁷***Then they laid hands on them, and they received the Holy Spirit.*

Once we get filled, we have eaten the head of the lamb in spirit. We have the mind of Christ. This is one of the reasons Paul said, "Let this (Christ's) mind be in you, just "let" it "be." We just have to digest the Head. We allow His thoughts, which are higher than our thoughts, to go through our mind and body to write a new mind in us.

SEALED WITH THE INK OF THE SPIRIT

2 Corinthians 3:2-3, NKJV **²***You are our epistle written in our hearts, known, and read by all men;* **³***clearly you are an epistle of Christ, ministered by us,* **written** *not with ink but* **by the Spirit** *of the living God, not on tablets of stone but on tablets of flesh, that is, of the heart.*

---

[8] See Luke 9:52 where Jesus called his disciples "messengers" (lit., angels); see also Luke 7:24 where John, the Baptist's disciples are also called messengers (lit., angels)

*Revelation 14:1, NIV: Then I looked, and there before me was the Lamb, standing on Mount Zion, and with him 144,000 who had **his name** and his Father's name **written** on their foreheads.*

How is the name of the Lamb written on the foreheads (minds) of the Believers? It is done with the ink of the Holy Spirit when we get baptized in the Spirit. Whichever way one looks at the mind of Christ, it is linked to the Holy Spirit. We do have the mind of Christ. However, this seal also has to be written on our mind (the two (minds) become one). In the words of Peter, the "same mind" as Christ!

According to Paul, the Spirit of the Lord is the "ink." This ink of the Spirit is applied by the "hands" of Jesus' ministers. "Clearly you are an epistle of Christ, ministered by us (Paul and the others)." A pen with its ink needs a "hand" to write. So likewise, the ink of the Spirit is applied by the hands of His "able" ministers.

Thus, the seal in Revelation, Chapter 7, the names written in Revelation, Chapter 14 were written by His ministers with the ink of the Spirit. This is why we must emphasize that we the Saints do not forsake the assembling of ourselves. The Spirit wants to write on the foreheads of His People (Ezekiel 9:1-11). He wants to complete the sealing. In the Old Testament, there were three seals on the High Priest.

He carried the sealed [living] stones on his chest—our salvation. He carried the sealed [living] stones on his shoulders—filled with the Holy Spirit. Finally, he wore the seal, HOLINESS TO THE LORD, on his forehead—we are sealed in our mind with the mind of Christ. This seal on his forehead is the same seal on the forehead of the believers in Revelation, Chapter 7, Chapter 9, Chapter 14, and so on.

According to Colossians, we are "holding fast to the **head**" — the **head** of the Lamb. We must eat the Lamb's head, the whole thing, and we must make it personal with the Lamb of God like the Lord in Moses exhorted the people to do. **"Your** lamb…eat it…roasted in fire — its head…" (Exodus 12:5-9).

THE LAMB'S FEET

John 1:29-36, NKJV: ²⁹*The next day John saw Jesus coming toward him, and said,* **"Behold! The Lamb of God** *who* **takes away the sin** *of the world! ...*³⁵*Again, the next day, John stood with two of his disciples.* ³⁶*And* **looking at Jesus as He walked,** *he said, "Behold the* **Lamb of God!"**

Exodus 12:5-9, NKJV: ⁵**Your lamb** *shall be without blemish, a male of the first year. You may take it from the sheep or from the goats....*⁹*Do not eat it raw, nor boiled at all with water, but roasted in fire – its head with its* **legs** *and its entrails.*

Every walk has a particular voice. Or the way a person walks usually makes a statement. A confident person walk is different from that of a person who has no self-confidence. John saw Jesus "walking," and as He was "looking" at Jesus walking, John concluded that Jesus was/is "The Lamb of God." What did John see in Jesus' walk? John saw a confident man who "carried" responsibility; yet he was/is approachable as a Lamb.

Consider now! This was said before the Lamb of God did any of His works. Also, the sign that John was to look for, as indicated by the voice of God to John, was the sign of the Holy Spirit descending like a dove and remaining on Jesus.

Yet, before the Spirit descended bodily onto Jesus, John saw a certain character in the walk of Jesus and called Him the Lamb. John had to have seen something in Jesus that prompted him to make the statement, "Behold the Lamb...." Something similar happened to the other John, John, the beloved.

LION/LAMB

Revelation 5:5-6, NKJV: *⁵But one of the elders said to me, "Do not weep. Behold, **the Lion** of the tribe of Judah, the Root of David, has prevailed to open the scroll and to loose its seven seals." ⁶And **I looked and** behold… a Lamb….*

The "elders" said that "the Lion…of Judah…has prevailed…." However, when John **looked** for the Lion, he saw "a Lamb." What does this mean? John, the Baptist saw a Lamb in Jesus' walk. John, the apostle also saw a Lamb when he should have seen a Lion. Every person has what I call "an impression of being."

Another way of saying this: Most of the time when there is interaction with a person "that which appears to the observation of understanding" concerning the person usually occurs. This is called in the common vernacular, "first impression." The "impression of being" concerning Jesus, whenever anyone meets Him, is that of a Lamb. Jesus was indeed a Lion, but He was seen as a Lamb. In other words, Jesus' public appearance was that of a Lamb. However, in His prayer life He is a Lion. This "lion-like" demeanor is of the Melchizedek Order.

*Hebrews 5:5-7, NKJV ⁵So also **Christ** did not glorify Himself to become High Priest, but it was He who said to Him:…"**You** are a priest forever According to the **order** of **Melchizedek**"; ⁷Who, in the days of His flesh, when He had offered up prayers and supplications, with **vehement ["loud" (NIV, NASU)] cries** and tears to Him who was able to save Him from death, and was heard because of His godly fear*

*Matthew 11:29, NKJV: Take My yoke upon you and learn from Me, for I am **gentle** and **lowly** in heart, and you will find rest for your souls.*

The statement in Hebrews shows Jesus as a Lion in prayer. The verse in Matthew shows Jesus in public as a Lamb. We must be "vehement" in prayer; and we must be gentle and lowly in public. Now "lowly" does not mean beaten down on the inside. "Lowly" (Greek, tapeinos) means, **not rising far from the ground,** lowly, of low degree, **lowly in spirit, humble"** (Thayer).

Our English word humble is from the Greek word "humas" or "humin" which means earth (as in real) or dirt. "Humas," and "humin" are used in the New Testament for "you," "your," "your own," "yourselves." Our English word "man" means human being, "human" (earth, dirt, you), and "being" (person, life). **Therefore being "lowly" is being "you."**[9] It has nothing to do with outward piousness.

My point is this: The "impression of being" they saw in Jesus as the Lamb of God was Jesus being **"himself."** He was humble. That is, He was down to earth. Jesus had **"depth of earth"** (Matthew 13:5). He was very "human" and very "God."

The Lamb nature was his "gentle" and "lowly" ("real") state. Yes! In prayer our Lord was like a Lion. However, in public he was as real as the earth. He could be touched. He was approachable. He was not puffed up with pride. He is the Lamb of God.

His Lion's character was shown in the fact that He is **"loud"** and "vehement" (lit.; forceful) in prayer. "Cries" is translated as "outcry." Thus, he did not muffle all His prayers. He was very loud and strong. It is not immature to pray with a loud voice.

It is said that when a Lion roars to establish his territory, he can be heard in a 5 miles radius. That's loud to me! If some people would hear some men and women of God pray the sound may scare them.

---

[9] Dr. Myles Monroe

Yet sometimes that is what it takes to be delivered from "death" — the last enemy to be rendered inactive.

*Hebrews 5:7, NKJV Who, in the days of His flesh, when He had offered up prayers and supplications, with **vehement cries** and tears to Him who was able to save Him from **death**, and was **heard** because of His godly fear,*

*Hebrews 5:7, NASU: In the days of His flesh, He offered up both prayers and supplications with **loud crying** and tears to the One able to save Him from **death**, and He was **heard** because of His piety.*

*Hebrews 5:7, NIV: During the days of Jesus' life on earth, he offered up prayers and petitions with **loud cries** and tears to the one who could save him from **death**, and he was **heard** because of his reverent submission.*

God does "hear" "loud" prayers. Yet, there are some who teach that we do not need to pray with a loud voice. I disagree. Sometimes you have to get "loud" with "death" himself. If Jesus prayed loud, and He did, so can we? The Lion of Judah got loud with death when He went to raise Lazarus from the dead.

*John 11:43-44, NKJV: 43Now when He had said these things, He cried with a **loud** voice, "Lazarus, come forth!" 44And he who had **died** came out bound hand and foot with grave clothes, and his face was wrapped with a cloth. Jesus said to them, "Loose him, and let him go."*

When our Lord faced the last enemy, death, He was not passive. He got "loud" with death and the dead. He conquered death with a "loud voice." In fact, He even did something rare in public contrary to His general custom, (Matthew 6:5-6) relative to raising Lazarus from the dead, He prayed for **all** to **hear** Him

*John 11:41-42, NKJV: 41Then they took away the stone from the place where the dead man was lying. And Jesus lifted up His eyes and **said**, "Father, I thank You that You have heard Me. 42And I know that You*

*always hear Me, **but because of the people who are standing by I said this,** that they may believe that You sent Me."*

The Lion must also be manifest in Prayer. We sometimes have to get "loud" against death; and the Father of the Lamb and His lambkin do hear loud prayers. However, the point still remains, Jesus walked as a Lamb in public. This is something that I had to learn in the Lord. "**Walk** in **wisdom** toward those who are outside…" (Colossians 4:5, NKJV).

The Lamb's nature is more attractive to the lost sheep than is a lion. This is why we are also instructed to eat the "legs" of the Lamb in Exodus 12:9. We must digest His earth walk—the lamb's legs are that which comes in contact with the ground. We must walk in His humility—being "down to earth" when it comes to relating with any person (poor or rich).

WISDOM WALK

*James 3:17, NKJV: But the wisdom that is from above is first pure, then **peaceable, gentle, willing to yield,** full of mercy and good fruits, without partiality and without hypocrisy.*

Wisdom from above is a walk. True wisdom is a lifestyle. It is not necessarily being "wise mentally." There are a lot of "wise fools" (sophomores). Wisdom is represented by how you live. In the words of Paul, "Wisdom from God" is also a Person.

*1 Corinthians 1:30, NKJV: But of Him you are in **Christ Jesus,** who became for us **wisdom from God** — and righteousness and sanctification and redemption*

The Lamb's walk was that of Wisdom from above. He was very peaceable, gentle, and willing to yield. His mercy is always "full" for all to appropriate. This is the walk of the Holy Spirit that Paul was alluding to. We are to "walk" like the Lamb "toward those who are outside" the kingdom of God.

1 Peter 2:21-23, NKJV: ²¹*For to this you were called, because Christ also suffered for us, leaving us an example, that you should **follow His steps**: ²²"Who committed no sin, Nor was deceit found in His mouth;" ²³who, when He was reviled, did not revile in return; when He suffered, He did not threaten, but committed Himself to Him who judges righteously.*

The Lamb's walk is not that of reviling in His response to being reviled. The Lamb's walk is that of suffering threats. There is no trickery in His walk. In the words of John, the Baptist: "Behold! The Lamb of God who **takes away the sin** of the world!" The Lamb's walk takes away sin. The Lamb's nature does not emphasize sin.

THE LAMB'S WALK TAKES AWAY SIN(S)

*Mark 15:20, NKJV: And when they had mocked Him, they took the purple off Him, put His own clothes on Him, and **led** Him out to crucify Him.*

*1 Peter 2:24, NKJV: Who Himself **bore** our **sins** in His own body on the tree, that we, having died to sins, might live for righteousness--by whose stripes you were healed.*

Jesus is an extraordinarily strong Man. He is not weak looking, like some have made Him. In fact, it is sin to make a picture, image, statue, or baby idol of Jesus. He is strong. Let me say it this way. Sin must have been very heavy for Him to **bleed** in the garden when He embraced His crucifixion (Luke 22:44).

He "bore" (lifted away) our sins. According to John the Baptist, the Lamb of God "takes away (lit.; lifts away) the sin of the world." He had to have strong legs to do that. We do not serve a weak Jesus. We serve the strong Lamb. His walk is attractive.

JOHN'S COMPLIMENT

John 1:35-38, NKJV: ³⁵*Again, the next day, John stood with two of his disciples.* ³⁶*And looking at Jesus* **as He walked,** *he said, "Behold the Lamb of God!"* ³⁷*The two disciples heard him speak, and they **followed** Jesus.*

The Lamb's walk caused two of the disciples of John to follow Jesus immediately. This is interesting. Whatever Jesus' walk looked like; it was attractive. There are also two principles that can be seen in the verses above. One, the walk of the Lamb will always attract followers—"they followed Jesus." Two, some disciples are only destined to follow their "John's" for only a time. In the right season, they will become a disciple to someone else. The person whom the disciple has left (to follow another leader) should not feel any inferiority or envy. It follows that the person who becomes the new teacher to that disciple should not gloat but walk gently before the Lord. It is also noteworthy to point out that John's disciples heard John compliment Jesus as the Lamb of God.

"The two disciples heard him [John] speak," and then "they followed Jesus." In other words, men of God should not be afraid to complement those who have the Lamb-like walk. There are so many insecure ministers. They refuse to build up other ministers. They are afraid the other minister will steal their flock. That is foolishness. The flock belongs to God; and if God gave you that group of people, no one can steal them. These are the days in which God is causing some to follow certain leaders for a season. They will then be directed to "follow" someone else for a time. The purpose is to bring them to maturity through the measure of another minister (Ephesians 4:7 w/4:11-13). John understood that the growth process is a corporate process (it takes more than one minister). In the words of Peter: "you [we] should **follow His** (their—Jesus' and John's—**steps.**"

THE LAMB'S ENTRAILS

*Exodus 12:5-9, NKJV: ⁵**Your lamb** shall be without blemish, a male of the first year. You may take it from the sheep or from the goats…⁹Do not eat it raw, nor boiled at all with water, but roasted in fire – its head with its legs and **its entrails**.*

*Matthew 9:36, NKJV: But when He saw the multitudes, He was **moved with compassion** (lit.; **intestine, bowels, spleen**) for them, because they were weary and scattered, like sheep having no shepherd.*

The word **"compassion"** has several meanings (intestine, bowels, and **spleen**, being a few). The **"spleen"** functions as that which filters the blood. There are also several meanings for the word **"entrails"** highlighted above in Exodus 12:9. "Entrails," as defined from the Hebrew means center, **nearest** part, innards. The root word for this word (entrails) means "to approach." "Entrails" is translated as **"in him."**

*1 Kings 3:28, NKJV: And all Israel heard of the judgment which the king [Solomon] had rendered; and they feared the king, for they saw that the wisdom of God was **in him** to administer justice.*

With the definitions above and the reference in 1 Kings 3:28, we can see truth concerning the Lamb of God. His "entrails" are the same as saying "in Him," as demonstrated above. **"In Him** all things consist" (Colossians 1:17b). **"In Him** all the fullness should dwell" (Colossians 1:19b). **"In Him** dwells all the fullness of the Godhead bodily." (Colossians 2:9), "and you (all of us) are complete **in Him"** (Colossians 2:10a). **"In Him** was life" (John 1:4). **"In Him** we live and move" (Acts 17:28a). "He (God) chose us **in Him** before the foundation of the world" (Ephesians 1:4a).

We must digest the "in Him" that is found throughout the Bible. The Lamb's entrails are important. There is righteousness in Him. It is important that we be "found **in Him,** not having my own righteousness" (Philippians 3:9a), but His righteousness.

APPROACH BOLDLY

Next, the word "entrails" also means "to approach." Thus, the entrails of Christ are that which causes us to approach God. He allowed His gut to be exposed and His flesh to be cut for us. He exposed His gut by "compassion" (as we will see in a moment), and He allowed His flesh to be cut for us to be able to approach God.

Hebrews 10:19-22, NKJV: [19]*Therefore, brethren, having* **boldness to enter** *the Holiest by the* **blood** *of Jesus,* [20]*by a new and living way which He consecrated for us, through the veil, that is,* **His flesh,** [21] *and having a High Priest over the house of God,* [22]*let us* **draw near** *with a true heart in full assurance of faith, having our hearts sprinkled from an evil conscience and our bodies washed with pure water.*

We can now approach God through the blood of the Lamb. Remember, one of the definitions for "compassion" is **spleen** — that which also acts as a filtration for blood. Therefore, His blood relates to His entrails. His "nearest parts" were exposed for us by the shedding of His blood. The ("center" of the) **"veil of the temple"** was ripped from top to bottom (Matthew 27:51), exposing that which was not lawful to be seen by all. So, likewise, the **"veil," that is His flesh"** was split, exposing his **innards** for us to approach God boldly, through His Blood. We must eat His entrails to partake of His bowels. In His bowels is compassion.

GUT FEELING – COMPASSION

*Matthew 9:36, NKJV: But when He saw the multitudes, He was **moved with compassion (lit.; intestine, bowels, and spleen)** for them, because they were weary and scattered, like sheep having no shepherd.*

You have heard of the saying, "go with your gut." Jesus did the same. The Lamb used his entrails regularly. He went with His "gut feeling" consistently. In the words of the Scripture: "He was **moved** with **compassion**" – the intestine, the belly, the bowels – for them."

Compassion comes from the innards. In this case, the compassion was for those who had no shepherd. He healed their sicknesses and diseases (Matthew 9:35). There is here an implied censure against those shepherds who do not want to see the flock healed but want rather to be in a constant state of dependency on the shepherd.

Jesus was the opposite of most today. The Lamb of God healed them. This is what a shepherd does for the flock. The Lamb carried the flock in His belly. He laid down His soul for the sheep. He is the Good Shepherd who is always looking for ways to add more laborers to or for His harvest.

Are we convinced that the compassion of healing, power and authority was given to the Lamb's kindred for harvesting the nations? The Lamb of God used it. Why do we not use the same tool to function as a shepherd for Jesus' flock?

We must have **"compassion"** for His flock. We must then **"move"** with this tool of **"compassion"** on behalf of the flock. Let the flock partake of the entrails (compassion) of Christ through His lambkins. Everyone must eat of the entrails (the compassion) of Jesus.

FORGIVENESS FROM THE GUT

Matthew 18:26-27, NKJV: ²³*Therefore the kingdom of heaven is **like** a certain king who wanted to settle accounts with his servants.* ²⁴*And when he had begun to settle accounts, one was brought to him who owed him ten thousand talents.* ²⁵*But as he was not able to pay, his master commanded that he be sold, with his wife and children and all that he had, and that payment be made.* ²⁶ *The servant therefore fell down before him, saying, 'Master, have patience with me, and I will pay you all.'* ²⁷*"Then the master of that servant was **moved with compassion**, released him, and forgave him the debt.*

*Luke 15:20, NKJV: And he arose and came to his father. But when he was still a great way off, his father saw him and had **compassion**, and ran and fell on his neck and kissed him.*

In Luke when the reckless son returned to his father, the father did not respond as most of us would have responded today. He did not curse him. He did not call to remembrance his wasteful life. No, The Father (God) **"had compassion"** on Him. The Father gave the son some entrails. What comes out of our "gut" in the season when the wasteful return home?

We are to **fall** on the **neck** and **kiss** those who have wasted the Lord's spiritual inheritance. Compassion is a powerful thing. Let us be conscious to forgive from the belly, not just from the lips. You never know when you may need the same "bowels of mercies" (Colossians 3:12, KJV; Philippians 2:1, KJV).

In Matthew, Chapter 18, a bond-slave (bond-slave of Christ) needed to be forgiven a large debt. He asked for "patience" from his "Lord" (God, Jesus) with respect to the repayment. Thus, his Lord "was **moved with compassion**, released him, and forgave him the debt."

The Lord gave His servant some of the Lamb's entrails. He gave him compassion, release, and forgiveness. God expects us to forgive others as He has forgiven us. However, this bond-servant did not know how to share. He thought the innards of compassion were only for him.

Later, a fellow bond-slave needed some of those entrails from him. The servant refused to share. He refused to be "moved with compassion." In fact, he choked his fellow servant. The end result was that that same servant, who was once forgiven a large debt, was now locked up, tormented, and required to pay all the debt.

*Matthew 18:28-35, NKJV: ²⁸But that servant went out and found one of his fellow servants who owed him a hundred denarii; and he laid hands on him and **took him by the throat**, saying, 'Pay me what you owe!' ²⁹"So his fellow servant fell down at his feet and begged him, saying, 'Have patience with me, and I will pay you all.' ³⁰"And **he would not**, but went and **threw him into prison** till he should pay the debt. ³¹So when his fellow **servants (or bond-slaves)** saw what had been done, they were very grieved, and came and told their master all that had been done. ³²Then his master, after he had called him, said to him, 'You wicked servant! I forgave you all that debt because you begged me. ³³Should you not also have had **compassion** on your fellow servant, just as I had pity on you?' ³⁴"And his master was angry and delivered him to the **torturers** until he should pay all that was due to him. ³⁵**So My heavenly Father also will do to you if each of you, from his heart, does not forgive his brother his trespasses."***

We are required to be moved with compassion from our bellies. We are required to forgive our fellow men. This is also for those whose parents, and grandparents were in bondage to slavery. You must forgive the former slave owners and their children.

COMPASSION FOR FELLOW SLAVES

Matthew 18:33, NKJV: **Should you not also have had compassion on your fellow servant (lit., slave),** *just as I had pity on you?*

John 8:32-36, NKJV: ³²*And you shall know the truth, and the* **truth** *shall* **make** *you free."* ³³*They answered Him, "We are Abraham's descendants, and have never been in* **bondage (lit., slavery)** *to anyone. How can you say, 'You will be made free'?"* ³⁴*Jesus answered them, "Most assuredly, I say to you,* **whoever commits sin is a slave of sin.** ³⁵*And a slave does not abide in the house forever, but a son abides forever.* ³⁶*Therefore if the Son makes you free, you shall be free indeed.*

Romans 8:15, NKJV: For you did not receive **the spirit of bondage (lit., the spirit of slavery)** *again to* **fear,** *but you received the Spirit of adoption by whom we cry out, "Abba, Father."*

First of all, slavery is a **"spirit of...fear."** According to Jesus, sinners are enslaved to sin, or sin is slavery. The Lord delivered us from the slavery of sin. In Matthew, Chapter 18 quoted earlier a slave was forgiven his sin; and it was expected that that forgiven slave would forgive his fellow slave.

This is the same for those who refuse to forgive others who enslaved them (Black slaves or White slaves). Without the Truth, all are slaves to sin (John 8:32-35). In Matthew, Chapter Eighteen, one slave (sinner) refused to forgive another slave (sinner), even though the Lord (Jesus) had forgiven one of the slaves. The result was prison for both and throat grabbing. This is also true for natural slavery. The more you take the children of the former slave owners by the "throat" and refuse to forgive them, the more assuredly you will be placed in "prison" (see Matthew 18:30-34 cited earlier).

Un-forgiveness is like taking someone by the throat, according to Matthew 18:28. The end result of this kind of abuse will be jail. Look at the youth of today. Yes, they are in prison for committing crimes. However, what is the real issue behind the crimes? Is it un-forgiveness because of being treated unfairly? Is it un-forgiveness towards fathers, mothers, brothers, uncles, aunts, and other races? Un-forgiveness will automatically cause a person (any person) to do things that could result in a prison sentence.

The reverse is also true for the children of the former slave owners, who are also fellow slaves to sin as well. Sin is a slave master. Therefore, any form of slavery is sin personified. They must repent (change their minds) of their mindsets toward the children of those whom they have enslaved or sinned against. They must forgive from the belly any grievances they may have against Black people of today. And I must add, I have met and know White men and White women who have reconciled with Black people. One of the results of real reconciliation is genuine fellowship.

The Father in heaven does not like it when we do not forgive one another, indicated by not fellowshipping with Churches of other races. Some may be considered as former slaves to others, yet all are former slaves to sin (John 8:34). The Church is not to be segregated. We are all from one blood (Acts 17:26) — the blood of the Lamb.

And for those who disdain the idea of being from one blood with people of other colors, in Christ, we are all from the same **Spirit** line. "There is neither Jews nor Greek [circumcised, uncircumcised, Black, Whites, Yellow, Brown, Tan, Mixed]," "slave nor free" "male nor female," "barbarian" (uncivilized according to "others'" standards), "For you are all **one** in Christ Jesus" (Galatians 3:28 w/Colossians 3:10-11).

There is "torture" and "prison" for those who refuse to forgive as God has forgiven them. There are many Whites, Black people, Chinese, Koreans, Spaniards, etc. who are in prison within their Churches, because they refuse to forgive from the belly. They are choking their fellow bond-slaves by total segregation.

There is no such thing as a Black church, or a White church. There can be a Church of India, or a Church of China. But there should not be a Church for Indians, only, or Chinese only. There is the Church of the living God of all nations. The Church must forgive from the belly and love each other from the belly. We expect God to forgive us for everything! Men and women must be moved with the same gut feeling of compassion as was found in Jesus. Some Churches in America are filled with people sitting next to people of other races with un-forgiveness in their hearts.

They go to their several houses and state why they cannot trust this Black Brother, or this White Brother, or this Jamaican Brother, this Latino Brother, this Chinese Brother, this Poor Brother. I was told by a Black Church leader that I was from "another [spiritual] seed" because I am a Jamaican. These practices ought not to be in the Church of the Living God!

There is only one "seed," Christ—"And if you are Christ's, then you are Abraham's **seed**, and heirs according to the promise" (Galatians 3:29, NKJV). Paul continued "…there is no distinction between Jew and Greek, for the same Lord over all is rich to all who call upon Him (Romans 10:12, NKJV). "There is no distinction between" races. This may sound strange to you, but from my youth I always had respect for all.

The first time I was impacted about the difference between races, I was about age twelve (12), and I was shocked! Shocked! It was so out of place to me. In Jamaica, I saw a Black youth doing something mean to a White person. I was so surprised by what happened, I asked him, "Why did you do that?" I may have been young and naïve relative to the era (1970s); however, my attitude was reconciliation, even from my youth.

There is so much restriction that the bowel of compassion (that is to flow through the Church) is stopped up. This could be one of the reasons there are no miracles. Compassion is one of the avenues by which God's power flows through His Church. Are we restricting ourselves?

We blame others for being responsible for some things we may have merited; or they may have rightly been guilty of. However, we restrict ourselves by closing our hearts to people. It is like a marriage. If the spouses do not forgive each other every time there is a disagreement, the marriage would not last. If they **withhold forgiveness,** it makes for a bitter companionship. You are not only restricted by people; you are restricted by your own gut feeling (unhealthy discernment).

RESTRICTED IN YOUR BOWELS

2 Corinthians 6:11-14, NKJV: ¹¹*O Corinthians! We have spoken openly to you; our heart is wide open.* ¹²*You are not restricted by us, but you are* ***restricted by (lit., in)*** *your own* ***affections (lit., intestine, spleen, bowels, entrails, compassion).*** ¹³*Now in return for the same (I speak as to children), you also be open.*

We have seen that the Lamb of God "moved with compassion" — His gut feeling. Thus, we have to make sure that our stomach is not stopped up with un-forgiveness. The Corinthians were restricted "in" their "bowels." In other words, they were "hemmed in" internally because of their own inabilities to release compassion properly.

The Corinthians claimed that they were being "restricted by Paul. Paul refuted that by saying **"You are not restricted by us."** Black Believers in America or any Believers (Whites, Latinos, Native Americans, etc.) from the so called First World, Second World or Third World countries must stop saying that certain Whites are restricting them. Freedom is on the inside of you. Freedom is internal knowledge of who you are through the enlightenment of Christ (John 8:32).

In other words, the "gut feeling" of mistrust is leading some to experience self-restrictions. It is a pseudo discernment and/or knowledge. Anything between your ears (your mind) telling you not to trust your Brother in the Lord is a lying entity. Most are restricting themselves by impure internal thoughts or the lying opinion of others. When you receive the compassion of the Lamb, all internal restrictions will leave. Even when someone is wronging you, you must not restrict them or yourself, but forgive.

Joseph (a Hebrew) was sold into slavery by his half-brothers. This is what happened to some Black people, some Aztecs, and some Whites centuries/millenniums ago. When Joseph was situated in Potiphar's house, Joseph became the number-one man in the house because the Lord was with him and Joseph "pushed forward" everything he did for Potiphar. He did not "restrict" himself, and he did not restrict what Potiphar was doing. He may have been a slave by Egypt's standard: however, he knew, internally, he was a "ruler" (Genesis 37:7-8, Genesis 41:40-45).

He was industrious in his apparent external restrictions. We need to have more Christians with this attitude of internal freedom and openness. No Believer should restrict their compassion but push forward in the things of God with the children of God regardless of race, or apparent temporary positions. Some Whites must not be afraid to submit to Black Leaders. Some Black Believers in the

Church must understand that slavery did not begin with them (the Black people replaced the Aztecs), and Black people must forgive the White race.

Also, do you know that one of the underlying reasons the Civil War in America was fought was because of slavery. The South wanted to keep it for economic reasons, the North wanted to abolish it for humane and constitutional[10] reasons. Therefore, in essence, White blood was shed for Black slaves.

Now, I understand that segregation still existed back then; and that it partially still exists today, and no race should submit to dehumanization. Yet, the point still remains, Whites also gave blood for Black people to be freed. We must look at both sides. **Some of the children of former slave owners must be transparent and submit to true interactions by repenting from enforcing the secret mentality of master and slave relationship.** The children of the slaves have to forgive the children of the slave owners.

The word "slave" was derived from the "Slavic" people, among the first Europeans to be enslaved. The Slavic are White. Colonization was not just with Black, Red, and Yellow peoples. The Whites colonized their own color. The Russians did this to their own color. To this day (2005) the Russians still have colonies in White countries. The British (a majority White nation) are subjugating the Irish (who are also White). The German also did this to people with the same color as themselves during World War II (i.e., the Polish Nation, German Jews, etc.).

With that said, I agree with what one of my apostolic supporters (who happens to be White) has indicated. He does not believe that

---

[10] Note: I am aware of the definition in the Constitution that was assigned to blacks during that era.

segregation in Churches and the world is only a "skin" issue. He believes it is a "sin" issue. Genesis and the book of Romans teach that the spirit of slavery is a result of sin. Thus, we must continually be "moved with compassion" as our Lord demonstrated. Yet, having compassion does not mean that a person should crouch to another race. This does not mean that one should become passive relative to who he/she is as a human being.

This does not mean that a person should roll over and be abused. Joseph was not bitter; and, at the same time of forgiving his brothers, he was not acting timid in their presence. Joseph was confident as a person. Joseph made sure his half-brothers were sincere before he gave himself to them. Things will happen to offend; yet you must be ready to move with the compassion of forgiveness. Do not restrict your bowels of compassion by holding onto the past.

Continuing with Joseph: Joseph's story was also lied about by Potiphar's wife and was sent to prison based on a lie of rape. This is happening to some Black people today and in the past. Societies (some Whites, some Chinese, some Mexicans, some Japanese, and some conditioned Black people) must stop the lies that are being propagated about Black people relative to crimes, land care, work ethics, and intelligence that are creating and building stereotypes.

Most people are now conditioned to believe that Black people are the worst criminals in America. However, according to the **"Uniform Crime Reports, US Department of Justice" (2003),** Whites have the highest percentage of total arrests for "offense charged" in all categories, except for one or two. Conciliation must occur through truth by Jesus Christ.

The misrepresented must however continue to be like Joseph. When he got to prison Joseph was put in charge, again. Why?

Joseph "pushed forward"—"prospered." Everything he did was his best for the race of those who mistreated him. He did not restrict his entrails of compassion. The Black people, some Whites, some Latinos, Chinese, etc., who are/were being mistreated must forgive from the heart. God will see to it that the resentful are **released** from natural and internal prisons when they forgive from the belly.

Ecclesiastes 4:13-14, NKJV: ¹³*Better a **poor** and **wise** youth…*¹⁴***For he comes out of prison to be king,** although he was born poor in his kingdom.*

Ecclesiastes 4:13-14, KJV: ¹³*Better is a poor and a **wise** child…*¹⁴*For **out of prison** he cometh to **reign**….*

Finally, because Joseph did not lose the dream the Lord gave him (Genesis 37:5-11), he was eventually placed as the second in power over Egypt because of his **"wisdom"** to organize and store. He came "out of prison…to reign." I believe, as we forgive our fellow man with bowels of compassion as Jesus and the Father forgave us, we will become leaders of men. We ought to be mature and use our strength for construction and not for destruction.

Joseph could have used the opportunity of rulership for revenge. Instead, Joseph said, "Do not be afraid, for am **I in the place** of God…**to save** many people alive." Neither Black people, Whites, Yellow, Brown should use power for revenge, especially, in the Church! Instead, Believers should be like Joseph. He forgot his past maltreatment. He also showed this by his son that was named Manasseh—"for God has made me **forget** all my toil and all my father's house" (Genesis 41:51).

We ought to use our bowels to push forward life. The Lamb of God forgave His own brothers (Jews) for killing Him. On the cross Jesus forgave the very ones who crucified Him. He found it in His gut to forgive while he was looking at the ones who just put Him on the cross. His entrails gave life in the midst of death. This is exactly what Joseph did to his half-brothers.

Genesis 50:17-21, NKJV: *¹⁷'Thus you shall say to Joseph: "I beg you, **please forgive** the trespass of your brothers and their sin; for they did evil to you." 'Now, please, **forgive** the trespass of the servants of the God of your father." And Joseph wept when they spoke to him. ¹⁸Then his brothers also went and fell down before his face, and they said, "Behold, we are your **servants**." ¹⁹Joseph said to them, "Do not be afraid, for am I in the place of God? ²⁰But as for you, you meant evil against me; but God meant it for good, in order to bring it about as it is this day, to save many people alive. ²¹Now therefore, do not be afraid; I will provide for you and your little ones." And he **comforted** them and spoke **kindly** to them.*

Joseph was a very compassionate man. He was just like the Lamb of God. He forgave them from his bowels. The very ones who sold him into slavery; the very ones who threw him into a pit, the very ones who hated him; the very ones who lied and said a beast killed him when it was his own brothers who sold him into slavery for death. He was not restricted in his affection. Imagine what Jesus had to do on the cross. Our Lord was a man of **no** "restriction."

He released His "affections" — His bowels of compassion. It is stronger to forgive; it is weaker to retaliate. Anger destroys; forgiveness from the gut builds up the Holy Nation and the nations. Do not forget! The ones who overcome in the Church of Jesus are destined to disciple, teach, and shepherd all nations (Matthew 28:19-20; Revelation 2:26-27). We must be like Jesus. We must forgive from the gut even in the midst of pain and suffering. On the cross Jesus said the following:

Luke 23:34a, NKJV: Then Jesus said, "Father, forgive them, for they do not know what they do."

The **"spleen"** acts as a **filtration** for **blood**. We should filter every offense against us, including **bloodshed,** through the "spleen" (compassion) of the Lamb. His entrails must be at work in us. Be reconciled with your Brothers and Sisters in the Lord as well as being reconciled with all races outside the Church. The Lamb was not a racist. He could have only died only for the people of His race — the Jews.

On the contrary, He died for all races. He removed the dividing wall between the races and genders (Galatians 3:28). We are fellow citizens of God's country with the saints and the household of God. There is one Body of Christ, one new man, not Churches fragmented by race. The Lord's bowel of compassion for all races was demonstrated on the cross. His "spleen" (compassion) is the filter for the blood of all nations. His blood is what causes the nations to be "brought near"

Ephesians 2:11-19, NKJV: *[11]Therefore remember that you, once Gentiles in the flesh--who are called Uncircumcision by what is called the Circumcision made in the flesh by hands — [12]that at that time you were without Christ, being aliens from the commonwealth of Israel and strangers from the covenants of promise, having no hope and without God in the world. [13]**But now in Christ Jesus** you who once were far off have been brought near **by the blood of Christ**... so as to create **in Himself one new man** from the two, thus making peace...[19]Now, therefore, you are no longer strangers and foreigners, **but fellow citizens** with the saints and members of the household of God*

Galatians 3:8-9, NKJV: *[8]And the Scripture, foreseeing that God would justify the Gentiles by faith, preached the gospel to Abraham beforehand, saying,* **"In you all the nations shall be blessed."** *[9]So then those who are of faith are blessed with believing Abraham.*

THE LAMB AND THE OPEN BOOK

*Revelation 5:1-6, NKJV: ¹And I saw in the right hand of Him who sat on the throne **a scroll written inside and on the back, sealed with seven seals.** ²Then I saw a strong angel proclaiming with a loud voice, "Who is worthy to open the scroll and to loose its seals?" ³And no one in heaven or on the earth or under the earth was able to open the scroll, or to look at it. ⁴So I wept much, because no one was found worthy to open and read the scroll, or to look at it. ⁵But one of the elders said to me, "Do not weep. Behold, the Lion of the tribe of Judah, the Root of David, has **prevailed to open the scroll** and to loose its seven seals." ⁶And I looked, and behold, in the midst of the throne and of the four living creatures, and in the midst of the elders, stood **a Lamb...***

The book of Revelation was once sealed in the right hand of Him who sits on His throne. No one was **"worthy"** to open this scroll that was sealed with seven seals, except for One Person. Yet, whatever these seals were, it took the "prevailing" strength of the Lion of Judah to open these seals. In addition, it was opened as He **"stood** a Lamb." The Lion was seen as the Lamb in order to open the scroll.

There is a lot here; and I will not try to explain all of it. However, before I discuss the open scroll. Let us look at the Lion/Lamb truth, again. The Lion prevailed, as was noted in an earlier Chapter. However, it was the Lamb that opened the book. It takes a Lion of Judah to conquer the book; but it takes a Lamb to open it. Dr. Kelley Varner, who mentored me for about 15 years and became as a father to me for about 4 years before his passing, beautifully brought out this truth that the book has to be conquered. This can be found in his notes on Joshua where he discussed Caleb conquering "book town."

BOOK TOWN

Joshua 15:13-17 NKJV: ¹³*Now to Caleb the son of Jephunneh he gave a share among the children of **Judah**, according to the commandment of the LORD to Joshua …*¹⁶*And Caleb said, "He who attacks **Kirjath Sepher** and takes it, to him I will give Achsah my daughter as wife."* ¹⁷*So **Othniel** the son of Kenaz, the brother of Caleb, took it; and he gave him Achsah his daughter as wife.*

Kirjath Sepher [City (of a) Book or **Book Town**] is one of the first cities that was conquered for Judah (the Lion).[11] It took Judah (the Lion) to conquer Book Town. "Othniel" means the force of God. Thus, it took the force of a lion of God (Judah) to conquer book town. This is similar to Revelation. It was the Lion of the tribe of Judah that prevailed to open the book in God's right hand of power.

Book Town is the Bible. It takes a lion's attitude to conquer the Bible. The book was sealed in God's right hand; and it was the Lion who prevailed to open "the little bible." Something similar happened in Judah's history.

In the days of Caleb Book Town was occupied by another; and the "force of God" — Othniel — took the City for Caleb. The Bible has to be conquered by a lion's nature before some inheritances will be realized. Jesus the Lion of God, the Lion of Judah prevailed to open the sealed book; and the Lion of Judah has several principles. Here are just two principles.

---

[11] Dr. Kelley Varner

First, Judah means praise, to celebrate, to worship. Therefore, the Lion of Judah is the Lion of Worship. The Lamb of God is the only One who has worshiped the Father as is expected. The Lion of Worship has prevailed to open the book. It follows that as we worship the Father, He will open Book Town to us. A Psalm of David said that God reveals His secrets on the harp (worship). We have to worship God in Spirit in order to prevail in the book. Book Town has to be conquered; and it is done through **"celebrating"** the Father and the Son.

Second the Lion of Judah that prevailed also points to the measure of the altar of God. This is seen in Ezekiel's Temple. There are many who approach Ezekiel's temple literally. However, if one studies the verses properly, they will see that Ezekiel's temple is also made like a person. This Person is foremost Jesus, the Lamb of God. Secondly, this person also includes the Body of Christ.

Ezekiel 43:13-17, NKJV: [13]*"These are the **measurements** of the altar in cubits (the cubit is one cubit and a handbreadth ....* [15]*The **altar hearth (lit., lion of God)** is four cubits high, with four horns extending upward from the **hearth (lit., lion of God)**.* [16] *The **altar hearth (lit., lion of God) is twelve** cubits long, **twelve** wide, **square** at its four corners;* [17] *the ledge, fourteen cubits long and fourteen wide on its four sides, with a rim of half a cubit around it; its base, one cubit all around; and its steps face toward the east."*

The "altar hearth" literally reads as the "lion of God." Thus, this altar is that of the Lion's measure. This altar hearth (lion of God) is twelve multiplied by twelve (12x12), or twelve square (12^2). Twelve squared equals one hundred forty-four (144). Thus, the "measure" of this altar is the "measure of the Man," (144) as discussed earlier in the book (see Rev 21). Jesus is this Lion of God. He is the altar of the hearth.

It is also noteworthy to say that "altar hearth" is defined as the "mountain of God." Thus the 144,000 on Mount Zion with the Lamb are those who have accepted the Lamb's sacrifice and have left all to walk in that measure of the Lamb's divine nature. The name of the Lamb and the Father in their mind also depicts that measure of maturity.

It follows that one hundred forty-four (144) of the altar is also the measure of the "lion of God." In other words, the only way to get to the measure of the Lion/Lamb (Jesus) is through the "stretching" (as measure means in Ezekiel 43:13) of the altar. Book Town can only be conquered by those who have allowed God to "stretch" them by "extending" them out on the Altar.

This altar (Ezekiel 43:13) of sacrifice will then be changed to the lion of God (Ezekiel 43:14-15). The same thing happened in Revelation, Chapter 5. Is He a Lion or a Lamb? Is Ezekiel's Altar a Lion of God or a mountain of God? Is it an altar of God or a lion of God? There is a **change** that comes in the "bosom' of the Father. In this altar was a "bosom." What greater place to hear the secrets of God (having the book opened to you) than in His bosom. This is the place where the Son **"is"** (John 1:18).

Book Town was conquered by Judah, whose standard is a Lion (Genesis 49:8-12). And it was the Lamb's nature that was seen opening the book. That is, the Lion prevailed, but it is the Lamb that opens the Bible to us.

WORTHY TO OPEN THE BOOK

There is a reason the Lamb opened the book and not the Lion. The book that was opened by the Lamb contained some severe Judgments. Therefore, the only one who is qualified to open (release) these written judgments was the One who has the Lamb's Nature.

If you are quick to call down judgment upon mankind, you will not be able to have the Bible opened to you. The Lamb is qualified to open the book because He died, first, for mankind. It is the same for those who desire to flow in apostolic and prophetic judgments. You must attain to the measure of the Lamb's nature, first.

*Revelation 5:9, NKJV: And they sang a new song, saying: "You are **worthy** to take the scroll, and to open its seals; **for** You were **slain**, and have redeemed us to God by Your blood.*

You are not qualified to release the judgments written until you die to your self-ambitions. You will not have the open book to use if you want to see people killed. Christ died for them. And God has a method of speaking to people to **turn** their soul from hell before He judges them. The Lamb of God was worthy because He was "slain" for you and me. Thus, He could open these severe judgments because of His Lamb's nature. He **"stood** a Lamb;" therefore He is "worthy to take the scroll and to open its seals."

OPEN BOOK

*Revelation 22:10, NKJV: And he said to me, "**Do not seal** the words of the prophecy of this book, for the time is at hand.*

There is a lie that is going around saying that the book of Revelation is for the future (after the rapture); and that the book is sealed. This could not be further from the truth. The angel told John not to seal this book. If it is written that the book is not sealed, be careful if you are trying to seal it.

*Revelation 22:18-19, NKJV: ¹⁸For I testify to everyone who hears the words of the prophecy of this book: If anyone **adds** to these things, God will **add** to him the plagues that are written in this book; ¹⁹and if anyone **takes away** from the words of the book of this prophecy, God shall **take*** *away his part from the Book of Life, from the holy city, and from the things which are written in this book.*

This should make one fear God. This is why I do not understand why some want to **"add"** to this book. They **"add"** by saying that the book of Revelation is sealed. It is a lie to say the book of Revelation is sealed.

On the contrary, the book of Revelation is open[12]. For anyone who dares to reseal the book of Revelation to be used for only the natural Jews, God will "**add** to him [male or female] the plagues that are written in the book." Some also **"take away"** from the book of Revelation.

Some "take away" the fact that this book is for the Church, past, present, and future. They "take away" from this book when they teach that the book of Revelation is for the natural Jews and not for the Church. Let us hear Jesus' opinion on for "whom" this book is and for "when."

Revelation 22:16, NKJV I (lit.; Ego), **Jesus,** *have sent My angel to testify to you these things in the* **churches***. I am the Root and the Offspring of David, the Bright and Morning Star."*

Jesus has an "ego" about this prophesy of the book of Revelations. Listen to our Lord: **"I Jesus** have sent My angel to testify to you these things in the **Churches ....**" His "ego" states that "these things" are "things in the Churches;" they are not for the natural Jews (Romans 2:28-29).

---

[12] The caution here is that there are many things in the Bible that we may never understand (Daniel 12:8; 2 Corinthians 12:4; Revelation 10:4).

The book of Revelation is for the Churches, through the Churches and in the Churches made up of Jews, Greeks, Chinese, Indians, Latinos and so on. Is this too simple? The "whom" the book of Revelation was written for is the Churches. The "when" that the book of Revelation is: "these things…must **shortly** take place;" "for the time is **near.**"

(In fact, some of the prophecies of the book of Revelation were being fulfilled during the season when John was given the prophecy. Some of the open seals are already historically fulfilled and shall be fulfilled again! The first open seal of the Rider (Jesus) and His white horse (the Church) has been fulfilled? Jesus and His Church have conquered, are conquering and shall conquer with no violence!)

Revelation 22:6: NKJV: Then he said to me, "These words are faithful and true." And the Lord God of the holy prophets sent His angel to show His servants the things which must **shortly** take place.

Revelation 1:3, NKJV: Blessed is he who reads and those who hear the words of this prophecy and keep those things which are written in it; ***for the time is near.***

Therefore, whomever has "taken away" the fact that the Church of Jesus is the one whom this book of Revelation was written for and testified to, God may "take away his part from the Book of Life (or "Tree of Life" according to the Majority and Alexandrian Greek Texts)…." Those who take this book from "the time is near" to put it only in a futuristic time may lose their part in the "Book of Life" or "Tree of Life" and "the holy City."

The Bible, including, but not limited to, the book of Revelation is an open book. It is not sealed to the people of God. God expects us to know certain things (John 3: 9-10). He sent His Holy Spirit to "guide us into (lit.; in) all truth" (John 16:13). To us "it has been given to **know** the **mystery** of the kingdom of God" (Mark 4:11a).

APOSTLES OF THE LAMB

*Revelation 21:14, NKJV: Now the wall of the city had **twelve foundations**, and on them were the names of the twelve **apostles of the Lamb**.*

*Ephesians 2:20, NKJV: Having been built on the **foundation** of the **apostles** and **prophets**, **Jesus Christ Himself** being the chief cornerstone,*

*Ephesians 3:3-5, NKJV: ³How that by **revelation** He made known to me the **mystery**...⁵which in other ages was not made known to the sons of men, as it has now been revealed by the **Spirit** to His holy **apostles** and **prophets**:*

Apostles and prophets are noted for their unique revelations from the Lord. Apostles and prophets are the people the Lord uses to release good understanding to the Church. The Book is open to apostles and prophets. The first twelve apostles are called "apostles of the Lamb." This is significant relative to their source of understanding.

It was the Lamb who opened the sealed book. The Lion prevailed; but it was the Lamb who opened the Book. The apostles of the Lamb can be looked at from several standpoints. The Lamb of God indeed own them. They are the apostles **of** the Lamb. They were also lambkins (**kindred** of the Lamb of God) by faith. The phrase "of the Lamb" is **"genitive"** in case, which means **source**.

The Lamb is their "source" — spiritual Father. Therefore, they are "kin" to Him. They are the apostles **of** the Lamb. Also, the truth that they are apostles' of the Lamb points to the Word of God being "opened" to them (It is the Lamb who is worthy to open the book that was once sealed).

In other words, "the spirit of wisdom and revelation in the knowledge of Him" is natural to apostles and prophets, who spend time with Jesus (Acts 4:13 w/Ephesians 1:17). One may say this is true for the original twelve, but not true for the other apostles. The Lamb's revelation is true for apostles who came after the original twelve, as well.

Remember, it was the Lamb of God who said to His apostles "the Spirit of truth…will take what is Mine (the Lamb of God) and declare it to you" (John 16:13-14). The things revealed by the Holy Spirit are the things opened by the Lamb of God. The Holy Spirit is the source and initiator. Revelation of the Spirit is the same as the Lamb is opening the Book to His apostles and prophets. Therefore, there are apostles of the Lamb who have revelation from the Holy Spirit. Let me say it another way; there is difference between those who pry for forbidden secrets from "their own spirits" (Ezekiel 13:3), and those to whom the Holy Spirit reveals the mysteries of God as the Lord sees fit.

Luke 10:22, NKJV: All things have been delivered to Me by My Father, and no one knows who the Son is except the Father, and who the Father is except the Son, **and the one to whom the Son wills to reveal Him."**

Son is the One who reveals the Father to His apostles and prophets. It is the Lamb's nature to open the mystery of Christ and the Father to His "Saints" through His holy apostles and prophets by His Spirit (Ephesians 3:4-5; Colossians 1:26; 2:2). Apostles and prophets must allow the Lamb to be their source of revelation. God broke through to Samuel with understanding (see Hebrew definitions for 1 Samuel 3:1). It was God who called Samuel, Moses, Paul, Jeremiah, Ezekiel, and so on. They did not pry into the "call." God called them. Let me say it this way.

It was the Lamb who opened the book to the apostle John, the beloved. The result of the revelation was a book written through John. Peter himself also had books through Him. The revelation of Jesus enabled him to write two (2) books—First and Second Peter. The revelation of the Lamb also produced books from the apostle Paul—Romans, Corinthians, Galatians, Ephesians, Philippians, Colossians, Thessalonians, and so on.

The same is true for apostles and prophets of today. Those who are "kin" to the Lamb of God by being "born of (lit.; out of) God" will have the Bible open to them; and books will be generated out of them through the Spirit of wisdom, which the Spirit received from the Lamb of God. The Lamb's kin are candidates for understanding the scroll that is now open to apostles and prophets, foremost (Ephesians 3:1-5; 2 Corinthians 12:1, 12:7), evangelists, pastors, teachers, and Saints thereafter (Acts 8:30-35; Colossians 1:26; Mark 4:10-11).

In case you did not know, the Greek word translated as Lamb, in the book of Revelation and once in the book of John, literally means "lambkin" (according to Strong's Concordance), "diminutive" of a male lamb, a male lamb as lifting (He lifts away the sin of the world). The Lamb of God who died for our sin has some "kin." They are called Saints, Believers, the House of God, the Church, and the like. We are not called **"lambs" (lit.; lambkin)** for no reason (John 21:15, last part). We are **like** Him in this world (1 John 4:17, last part). "I (Jesus) send you forth **as** lambs…" (Luke 10:3, NKJV).

SILENCED LAMB?

*Mark 15:2, NKJV: Then Pilate asked Him, "**Are You the King** of the Jews?" And He answered and said to him, "**It is as you say.**"*

*Mark 15:4-5, NKJV: ⁴Then **Pilate** asked Him again, saying, "Do You answer **nothing**? See how many things they testify against You!" ⁵But Jesus still answered **nothing**, so that Pilate marveled.*

*1Timothy 6:13-15, NKJV: ¹³I urge you in the sight of God who gives life to all things, and before Christ Jesus who **witnessed** the **good confession** before **Pontius Pilate**, ¹⁴that you keep this commandment without spot, blameless until our Lord Jesus Christ's appearing, ¹⁵which He will manifest in His own time, He who is the blessed and only **Potentate, the King of kings and Lord of lords.***

The confession of Jesus before Pilate was twofold.: First, in the context of Paul writing the "good confession" of Jesus Christ is the Lamb of God not denying His "Potentate" (Greek: dunastes (lit., dynasty)). Second, His good confession also has to do with being silent as the Lamb before the shearer. He was indeed silent, but not silenced by men's pulpits.

SILENT, BUT NOT SILENCED

"Potentate," according to Paul, has to do with being King of kings and Lord of lords. Jesus' dynasty is forever. He **destroyed** the "dynasty" of the Devil, (Acts10:38—"oppressed" (Greek: **katadunasteuo** means "to exercise a dynasty" or to throw down a dynasty). Jesus is the "only Potentate." He is King over everyone and everything. Jesus did not deny His Kingship before Pontus Pilate. **"Pilate asked..."Are you King...He answered...'It is as you say.'"**

The Lamb was not afraid to confess who He is before any earthly ruler. He did not deny but confessed (compare John 1:19-23) that He (Jesus) is indeed King of the Jews (spiritual Jews and natural Jews) (Romans 2:28-29). How is this significant for the Believer? What does this mean for me today?

The answer is this: At the moment that Jesus was asked the question concerning His Kingship, what state was He in? He was bound. He had been abused physically. He was not on a natural throne. He was in a state of depravation. He appeared to be weak.

Yet, in spite of His state contrary to the pomp of royalty, He still agreed with the statement of Pilate. "Are You **the King** ...?" And [Jesus] answered..."**It is as you say.**" Yes! He is "the King;" even though His natural circumstances just before His crucifixion were contradictory.

This is a good confession for all Believers to declare. What is contrary to your dominion that was restored to you by the Lamb? The Lamb was silenced by God, but not silenced by man's apparent pseudo authority. There is "A time to keep silence" as we will see in a moment. However, there is also **"a time to speak"** (Ecclesiastes 3:7b).

With regard to Pilate's statement, it was "time" for the Lamb of God "to speak." The time to speak is when men or the spirit of the world try to question the King's domain and His Churches' rulership. Jesus was not silent or silenced when it came to His Kingship, as seen in the book of John. John's account was a little more assertive than Mark's. Listen to the beloved John.

*John 18:37, NKJV: Pilate therefore said to Him, "Are You a king then?" Jesus answered, "**You say rightly that I am a king**. For this **cause** I was born, and for this cause I have come into the world, that I should bear witness to the truth. Everyone who is of the truth hears My voice."*

Did you hear that assertion by the Lamb of God? **"You say rightly that I am a king."** The Lamb was not intimidated. He would not be silenced by any earthly ruler concerning His Kingship. We must be the same. In the face of persecution and contradiction, as to who we are in Christ, we must not deny our royal priesthood. We may not dress like it; some may currently not have earthly palaces; yet we are still "kings and priest to our God."

We should carry ourselves as we are rulers (dominators) — "Let Us [the Godhead] make man in Our image, according to Our likeness; let them have **dominion**..." (Genesis 1:28). Jesus' circumstances did not rule His mouth. His mouth **dominated** His circumstances. Jesus' confession so impressed Pilate that he had to confess the same concerning Jesus. And Pilate's confession was written down unable to be reversed.

*John 19:19-22, NKJV: [19]Now **Pilate wrote** a title and put it on the cross. And the writing was: JESUS OF NAZARETH, **THE KING** OF THE JEWS. [20]Then many of the Jews read this title, for the place where Jesus was crucified was near the city; and it was written in Hebrew, Greek, and Latin. [21]**Therefore the chief priests of the Jews said to Pilate, "Do not write, 'The King of the Jews,' but, 'He said, "I am the King of the Jews."'"**[22]Pilate answered, "What I have written, I have written."*

Pilate was bound by Jesus' confession. He had no choice but to write what Jesus' mouth declared. Even when the Jews who crucified Him asked to change Pilate's confession, Pilate refused to. He said, "What I have written, I have written." The same is true for us.

We define ourselves by our confession. Even if we die confessing our royal priesthood, our confession will be recorded in writing; and our enemy cannot change the truth. The Lamb witnessed such a "good confession" before Pilate that Pilate believed it and wrote it. The strength of our Lord's confession forced the hand (writings) of Pilate.

You are a king in the Lord; you are a royal priest from God; **and sometimes that definition of who you really are is not written about you until you are crucified (I learned this statement from my wife, Judith).** Jesus was defined to be King on the cross by the power of His confession. Saying it another way, you are not defined as to who you really are until you realize you were crucified with Christ. The cross will cause men to acknowledge (write) who you really are.

Mark 15:39, NKJV: So, when the centurion, who stood opposite Him, saw that He cried out like this and breathed His last, he said, **"Truly this Man was the Son of God!"**

The centurion realized that Jesus is the Son of God after the Lamb's death on the cross. Embracing your cross (Matthew 16:24) will cause the "centurion" — enforcers of the beast system of that time — to see your true identity. The cross also makes you one with the person and character of Christ. That is, your true definition is that of "Christ" — an anointed ruler in the Lord.

1Corinthians 12:12, NKJV: For as the body is one and has many members, but all the members of that one body, being many, are one body, **so also is Christ.**

Galatians 2:20, NKJV: I have been crucified with Christ; it is no longer I who live, but **Christ lives in me;** *and the life which I now live in the flesh I live by faith in the Son of God, who loved me and gave Himself for me.*

Christ lives in you when you embrace your crucifixion with Jesus. Who is Christ? Christ is the Messiah — the anointed one (John 4:25). If we are "crucified with Christ," we (plural) are also defined as messiahs — anointed ones (I Corinthians 12:12). Christ is "the Son of God" (Luke 4:41). We are sons of God (John 1:12). Christ is the Savior (John 4:42). We are also "saviors" (Obadiah 21). Christ is King and Lord (Luke 2:11, John 18:35); and He is King of **kings** and Lord of **lords** (Revelation 19:16).

My point, whatever the Lamb is, we are the same because we were crucified with Him. In other words, the "dominion" that we lost through Adam's "transgression" (lit.; to walk contrary, or to side-step) was restored to us through the cross of Christ. Christ is God who restored our God-given dominion. "Bills, fear, sex, our history, sin, and the like should not dominate us. We should dominate our "bills," dominate our history, exercise self-control, dominate sin, etc.

We are not slaves to sin anymore. We are princes on horsebacks through the cross of Jesus (Ecclesiastes 10:7). We ought to be thankful always for what the Lord did for us, through His sweat and blood! Thanksgiving to His name, or confessing His name is "fruit" (Hebrews 13:15) Thanks to Jesus, the Lamb of God who restored us through His Blood.

Therefore, do not let the pressure of the "offense of the cross" of Jesus cause you to change your confession. Jesus endured "contradiction of sinners" (Hebrew 12:4, KJV). It is sinners who speak against the Ruler in you (James 2:7). Do not allow the spirit of the world to change your good confession. Do not let your spirit crouch beneath the pressure of the world. Stand up and be of good cheer, even in the face of pressure.

The second part of His good confession is: His good confession also has to do with Jesus not opening His mouth "as a lamb to the slaughter." As noted above, this does not mean that you do not speak up to bear witness to the truth. Yet, there is a time to keep silent; while at the same time not being silenced by men, but by God.

SILENT

*Ecclesiastes 3:7, NKJV: …A **time** to keep silence….*

*Acts 8:32, NKJV: ³²… "He was led as a sheep to the slaughter; and **as a lamb before its shearer is silent**, So He opened not His mouth.*

*Mark 15:4-5, NKJV: ⁴Then **Pilate** asked Him again, saying, "Do You answer **nothing**? See how many things they testify against You!" ⁵But Jesus still answered **nothing**, so that Pilate marveled.*

At this point before His crucifixion, it was "time" for Him "to keep silence." Why did our Lord keep silent at this point? He could have caused all of His accusers to "draw back" and "fall" again if He chose (John 18:4-6, NKJV). He could have accepted His disciples on their request to fight for Him, yet He told them "to permit even this" (His arrest and eventual crucifixion) (Luke 22:48-51, NKJV).

He could have prayed to His Father (our Father also) to "provide…more than twelve legions of angels" to fight for Him (Matthew 26:52-53). However, He had a reason to keep silent. The motivation was: The Scripture had to be fulfilled.

*Matthew 26:54, NKJV: How then could the **Scriptures** be **fulfilled**, that it **must** happen **thus**?"*

Immediately after, He chose not to call the angels to defend Him, and He stated the reason. The Scriptures must be fulfilled. **"It must happen thus."** The Lamb kept silent because it was time to fulfill that which "must happen thus." Let me show you a sample of the great length to which the silent Lamb went to fulfill the Scripture.

Luke 22:36-38, NKJV: ³⁶*Then He said to them, "But now, he who has a money bag, let him take it, and likewise a knapsack; and* **he who has no sword, let him sell his garment and buy one.** ³⁷*For I say to you that this which is written must still be accomplished in Me: 'And He was numbered with the transgressors.' For the things concerning Me have an end."* ³⁸**So they said, "Lord, look, here are two swords."** *And He said to them, "It is enough."*

Before Jesus' arrest, He reminded His disciples to buy a sword. Jesus said, "He who has no sword, let him sell his garment and buy one." This statement was said in the context of the Scripture being fulfilled — **"For (Greek: Gar (because)** I say to you that this which is **written** must still be accomplished **in** Me."

Jesus reminded them to bring the swords; and told then to buy a sword if they did not have one; "because" the Scriptures "must be accomplished in Him." In other words, the Lamb of God reminded them to bring swords to fulfill the Scriptures, even though; He will eventually rebuke them for using them.

The events in the garden had to go a certain way. It had to be fulfilled that Peter would cut off the ear of one of the high priest's servants so that Jesus would have the opportunity to immediately heal. This act being fulfilled was so crucial for Jesus that He reminded them to bring the swords. He went through great lengths to fulfill every Scripture. What does that mean for us today? It means that even in the midst of unjust persecution, we should still bring healing, as the Lamb did for the man's ear. It also means that we must be meticulous enough to fulfill all Scripture written about us (His Church).

Jesus had the same attitude about His crucifixion. Because it was time to be silent, He did not open His mouth to prevent His crucifixion. The Scripture had to be fulfilled! Jesus was predestined to suffer tribulations and be crucified.

There are some people who are trying to enter the kingdom of God without suffering. They always speak their way out of sufferings. They are not fulfilling the Scriptures that say, "We **must** (lit.; necessary as binding) through **many tribulations** enter the kingdom of God" (Acts 14:22, last part, NKJV). Suffering is part of the Christian walk. There is no way to get out of suffering, except by going through suffering. We enter the Kingdom of God through the many pressures. "For, in fact, we told you before when we were with you that **we would suffer tribulation,** just as it happened, **and you know**" (1 Thessalonians 3:4, NKJV).

Anyone who belongs to God and does not suffer is playing with his/her entrance into the kingdom of God or the King's (God's) domain. Suffering also causes us to cease from sin (1 Peter 4:1). Those who refuse to suffer tribulation must not plan to stop sinning. We must allow the Scriptures [Acts 14:22] to be fulfilled in our life. Jesus embraced His cross; and we are admonished to do the same. The Lamb kept silent when it was time for him to partake of the ultimate suffering.

"Jesus…answered **nothing**" that the Scriptures might be fulfilled. We must learn, as Believers, to endure suffering quietly as the Lord wills for us. How many times have our souls cursed God because we were suffering something that was inexplicable at the time? Why did we not quiet our souls?

Psalms 13:2, NKJV: Surely, I have calmed and **quieted my soul,** *like a weaned child with his mother; like a weaned child is my soul within me.*

David learned the Lamb's nature. He learned to quiet his soul. Are we loud talking God? Are we stronger than God? Who are we to "speak" when God says, "it is a time to be silent." We must be like the Lamb of God. We must know when to speak and when to keep silence.

THE LAMB AND THE POOR

*Luke 4:18, NKJV: "The Spirit of the LORD is upon Me, **because He has anointed Me to preach the gospel to the poor....**"*

The Lamb of God's anointing was manifested in six (6) ways according to Luke 4:18. The first of the six (6) was to preach to the poor. The first work of the anointing is for the poor. This was also demonstrated by the apostles in the early Church. Paul was admonished to remember the poor (Galatians 2:10). It takes the anointing to be concerned about the poor. The Lamb of God was "anointed" to preach to the poor.

THE POOR NEEDS ...

*Matthew 11:4-5, NKJV: ⁴Jesus answered and said to them, "Go and tell John the things which you hear and see: ⁵The blind see and the lame walk; the lepers are cleansed and the deaf hear; the dead are raised up and **the poor have the gospel preached to them.***

In the verse above we see several needs of the people. The blind need sight. That is a very logical conclusion, yes! The lame need the ability to walk. This is another logical conclusion, is it not! The lepers need to be cleansed. This makes sense.

The deaf need hearing: this is also true. The dead need to be made alive again. This all make sense in the logical brain. It follows that the poor need money, right? The answer is no! The poor do not primarily need money. The poor need "the gospel preached to them." This literally means that "the poor is evangelized." Yes, Jesus evangelized the poor demonstrating God's love for all.

Thus, giving the poor money is not the only solution. The issue is that they need the gospel preached to them. Jesus Himself said this.

The next logical question is should we or should we not give money to the poor? The answer is yes! That depends on the situation as we will see later. Nonetheless, Jesus indicated that the need of the poor is the gospel, not necessarily money. What then is the gospel?

THE GOSPEL

The gospel is named as follows: The gospel of Christ, or Jesus Christ (Romans 1:16; Mark 1:1); the gospel of God (Romans 15:16); the everlasting gospel (Revelation 14:6); the gospel of peace (Romans 10:15. Ephesians 6); the gospel of your salvation (Ephesians 1:13); the gospel of the grace of God (Acts 20:24); the gospel of the kingdom, etc. As one can see the gospel encompasses many facets. Yet, what is the gospel? "The gospel," according to Jesus, is that "the kingdom of God is at hand."

Mark 1:14-15, NKJV: [14]*Now after John was put in prison, Jesus came to Galilee, preaching* **the gospel** *of the kingdom of God,* [15]*and saying,* **"The time is fulfilled, and the kingdom of God is at hand.** *Repent, and believe in the gospel."*

The gospel that Jesus preached was "the gospel of the kingdom of God...**saying,** the time is fulfilled, and the **kingdom of God** is at hand." "The gospel" is the gospel of the King's dominion the King's statute). The poor need to know that the crushing of mankind's spirit is now at an end—the time is fulfilled for the King's dominion, the King's law of the Holy Spirit of life.

The King's dominion/rule/control is now at hand. The poor do not only need money. The poor also needs to know how to dominate by their spirit through the Holy Spirit! Saying it another way, most who have money have learned the mystery of dominating through their spirit. One of the Lamb's concern was to "perfect" the poor spirits of men and women.

THE POOR IN SPIRIT

Matthew 5:3, NKJV: **Blessed** *are the* **poor in spirit,** *for theirs is the kingdom of* **heaven.**

Luke 6:20, NKJV: Blessed are you **poor,** *for yours is the kingdom of* **God.**

Matthew 11:5, NKJV: … The **poor** *have the* **gospel** *preached to them.*

"Poor" is defined as pauper (**non- productive**), **to crouch**, and to be beggarly, etc. A "crouching" spirit causes poverty. "Poor" is also defined as those who **"do not know the way of the Lord" (Jeremiah 5:4-5).** One of the reasons the poor are also poor is because their spirits are underdeveloped.

Those with poor spirits are poor financially because their spirits are weak. Their spirits are weakened by the oppression of sincere but ignorant parents, excessive oppression of bullies, being discouraged by teachers misplace assessments, economics systems, demonic oppression, rape stigmas, sexual violations, etc.

Thus, for the most part, when the spirit is developed, poverty can be dealt with. The foremost way ones spirit is developed is by love [(God's love for us, and pure love from fellow humans), 1 John 3:16]. The Lamb's good news to the "poor in spirit" is that they also have a place in Jesus; and they also have God's love with them.

In other words, the poor need to understand the good news that all of mankind was created to rule in life, through God; and if the poor can understand <u>their</u> heavenly origin and place in Christ, they can rule in life. As Jeremiah indicated, understanding "the way of the Lord" (including the "Way" of the Lord's kingdom) is a key. The poor in spirit are as **"blessed"** as all other person on earth.

"**Blessed**" is from a Greek root word that means "lengthy" or "large" (see Vines Dict.). This is significant. The crushed spirit needs to be lengthened. Remember that poor means "to crouch." Thus, through "crouching," the spirit is shortened. This is a direct result of the spirit of slavery (Romans 8:15). Slavery in general or slavery to sin shortens or bends the spirit of man.

*Exodus 6:9, NKJV: So, Moses spoke thus to the children of Israel; but they did not heed Moses, because of **anguish (lit.; short) of spirit** and cruel bondage (lit.; severe work).*

*Proverbs 14:29, KJV: He that is slow to wrath is of great understanding: but he that is **hasty (lit.; short) of spirit** exalts folly.*

The children of Israel were enslaved in Egypt. The result of this slavery was a **"short** (crouched) spirit." Other men ruled them, contrary to God's plan for mankind. Paul says, **"...do not become slaves of men." (I Corinthians 7:23).** Solomon also says that when a man rules over another man, it will turn to his own hurt. There is a time in which one man **rules** over another[13] to his own **hurt** (Ecclesiastes 8:9, NKJV)

This is what happened to Pharaoh and his people. God hurt them for refusing to free the slaves. The same is true today (2005) for the nations who are enslaving people. Enslaving others will eventually hurt those who enslave. Nonetheless, the spirits of the people were shortened because of slavery. Some in the Black race and some Whites in Europe, America, etc. to this day have a shortened spirit because of the effect of slavery.

---

[13] This verse may also relate to marriage. A woman's spirit is called "man" (1 Peter 3:4). Thus, when the male man "rules" or dominates the female man, or vice versa, there will be "hurt" physically and spiritually in that marriage.

Slavery to sin does the same. It causes a person's spirit to be shortened or underdeveloped. According to Proverbs, a short, spirited person exalts folly or perversity. The spirit of slavery makes you crouch (poor) in spirit. This is why Jesus preached the good news of His dominion over sin or any other entity that dominates humanity. Why? We were not created to rule the spirits of men.

Jesus knew this; and His compassion for the poor (poor in spirit) was to teach them about their God-given dominion. He wanted their God-given spirits to be **"lengthened"** with a **large** vision. He "blessed" — lengthened, enlarged — the poor in spirit. The poor in spirit have to understand that **"the profit of the land is for all"** (Ecclesiastes 5:9a). The poor can rule the earth and the things of the earth like any other person, through Jesus. The poor whose spirits are developed can profit from the resources of the land. Poor African nations need to turn to the Lord for right[14] spiritual development in order to profit from their lands.

Any who are poor in the undeveloped nations, the developing nations and the developed nations must understand that they are also redeemed from the curse of the land (contrast Galatians 3:13 w/Genesis 3:17-19). The Lamb of God now "blesses" poor. Part of Jesus' anointing was to get the poor out of poverty by preaching the gospel of the kingdom to them. He was perfecting their spirits.

---

[14] It appears to me that poverty in some African nations and some Island nations is <u>partly</u> due to their spirits being underdeveloped from seeking ancestral spirits (Why seek the dead on behalf of the living) (Isaiah 8:19, NKJV)?], rather than seeking Jesus who is able to develop the spirit of the living.

PERFECTED SPIRITS OF MEN AND WOMEN

*Hebrews 12:22-24, NKJV: 22But you have come...to **the spirits of just men made perfect,** 24to Jesus....*

Our spirits also have to be "perfected." This perfection has to do with our crouching spirits standing up again. The perfected spirit is the resurrected spirit.

*Luke 13:32, NKJV: And He said to them, "Go, tell that fox, 'Behold, I cast out demons and perform cures today and tomorrow, and the third day I shall be **perfected.**'*

Jesus' reference to His third day **perfection** was His resurrection. On the third day He was resurrected. Resurrection means to stand up again (Strong's Concordance NT: 386). Therefore, the spirits of just men who were perfected are those whose spirits stood up again. In other words, their spirits were once poor, or crouched, non-productive, being dominated rather than dominating, but now their spirits are standing up again.

The gospel of the kingdom does this for the believers. It causes their spirit to stand in dominion. The Lamb of God was genuinely concerned for the poor. He wanted to develop their poor spirits by preaching to them "the gospel" of dominion. Let us see some examples of dominion over the earth.

THE LAMB'S DOMINION

Matthew 17:24-27, NKJV: 24When they had come to Capernaum, those who received the temple tax came to Peter and said, "Does your Teacher not pay the temple tax?" 25He said, "Yes." And when he had come into the house, Jesus anticipated him, saying, "What do you think, Simon? From whom do the kings of the earth take customs or taxes, from their sons or from strangers?" 26Peter said to Him, "From strangers." Jesus said to him, "Then the sons are free. ²⁷**Nevertheless, lest we offend them, go to the sea, cast in a hook, and take the fish that comes up first. And when you have opened its mouth, you will find a piece of money;** *take that and give it to them for Me and you."*

The temple tax had to be paid. Jesus, whose Spirit is already perfected, did not crouch to the demand of the temple tax collectors. Neither did He "beg" for the money. His spirit dominated in the circumstance. He asked His disciple Peter to go to the sea and catch a fish.

He then stated that the required money would be in the fish's mouth. Jesus declared what would happen and it did happen just as he said. He used His "spirit words" (John 6:63) to dominate the fishes according to Genesis 1:26. The first thing God gave man to dominate was the fish.

The poor (crouching, beggarly, non-productive) spirit would have buckled under the pressure of attaining the temple tax. Instead, the Lamb of God dominated His circumstance through the "word of faith." He partook of the "profit of the land (sea)." The Lamb spoke what He wanted to happen; and it did! The same happened to a tree that was non-productive (poor) towards Jesus. He dominated it!

Mark 11:12-24, NKJV: ¹²*Now the next day, when they had come out from Bethany, He was hungry.* ¹³*And seeing from afar a fig tree having leaves, He went to see if perhaps He would find something on it. And when He came to it, He found nothing but leaves, for it was not the season for figs.* ¹⁴*In response Jesus said to it,* **"Let no one eat fruit from you ever again."** *And His disciples heard it ...* ²⁰*Now in the morning, as they passed by, they saw the fig tree dried up from the roots.* ²¹*And Peter, remembering, said to Him,* **"Rabbi, look! The fig tree which You cursed has withered away."** ²²*So Jesus answered and said to them,* "*Have faith in God.* ²³*For assuredly, I say to you, whoever says to this* mountain, 'Be removed and be cast into the sea,' and does not doubt in his heart, but believes that those things he says will come to pass, **he will have whatever he says.** ²⁴*Therefore I say to you, whatever things you ask when you pray, believe that you receive them, and you will have them.*

Jesus dominated the trees of the field also. The fig tree should have had figs on it based upon its leaves. However, He did not waste words. He commanded the tree to never be eaten from again; and His words came to pass exactly as He said. He then compared His dealing with the tree to a mountain being removed.

This is strong; but we also have dominion over the mountains to move them if necessary. The problem is humanity's spirits are shortened because of sin. Yet, that is not true for believers (Romans 6:14). We rule the spirit of slavery. The spirit of slavery does not rule us. We rule the earth and the creatures of the earth. This rule must become manifested reality as the Lord perfects our spirits.

Those with short spirit or crouched spirits must be perfected through Jesus. He did not beg; He commanded the very provision of the earth. The Lamb also demonstrated His dominion over the wind and the sea. The wind ceased at His word. The Lamb has the ability to make the sea "smile." He also has authority over its buoyancy. He does not bend to adversity from any of the heavens, the earth, or under the earth.

*Mark 4:38-39, NKJV: ³⁸But He was in the stern, asleep on a pillow. And they awoke Him and said to Him, "Teacher, do You not care that we are perishing?" ³⁹Then He arose and rebuked the wind, and said to the sea, "Peace, be still!" And the wind ceased and there was a great **calm**.*

*Matthew 14:25-29, NKJV: ²⁵Now in the fourth watch of the night **Jesus went to them, walking on the sea.** ²⁶And when the disciples saw Him walking on the sea, they were troubled, saying, "It is a ghost!" And they cried out for fear. ²⁷But immediately Jesus spoke to them, saying, "Be of* *good cheer! It is I; do not be afraid."* ²⁸*And Peter answered Him and said, "Lord, if it is You, command me to come to You on the water."* ²⁹ *So He said, "Come."* **And when Peter had come down out of the boat, he walked on the water to go to Jesus.**

It is my prayer for the Church of Jesus Christ that "we" (yes! All of us, including me) would appropriate our God-given authority. When there was not a boat, He walked on water. His "spirit of faith" (2 Corinthians 4:13) was fully perfected. He did not crouch to the fact that He could sink. No! On the contrary His Spirit rules the seas also. In Mark, the Lamb told the wind and water to obey Him. And obviously, the water was in some kind of distress because the Scripture states that the sea **"smiled"** after He called for peace over the wind and water.

The word **"calm"** (by the Greek definition, Vine's Expository Dictionary) also means "to smile." There is a lot in this. When the poor in spirit are perfected in spirit by walking in the King's (God's) dominion, the creation will "smile" over its release from turmoil (Romans 8:19-23). The same is also true for the poor in spirit when the Lamb of God confirms their identity. Their spirits leap on the inside. A joy comes to the heart! Smiling instead of horror is produced because their spirits are functioning as the Lord created them!

Moses found this function of man's authority through the word of God. Moses crouched until God perfected him. The Lord God caused Moses' spirit to stand up again by telling him that Moses would be a God to Pharaoh (see Exodus 4:10-16).

The word of God was so powerful in Moses' perfected spirit that water could come out of a rock. The sea was parted; the heavens rained manna, which the Bible also equates to money. The earth opened and swallowed his enemies. Moses and other "great" men were not listed as an example because they were better than we are. The opposite is true. They are examples because they were like you and me. Their spirits had to be perfected just as ours have to be.

James said that Elijah was a man of like nature, just as we are (James 5:17). The same can be said for Elisha. The anointing (the Holy Spirit) that was in **them** caused oil to multiply. They opened the Jordan River, stopped rain, called for rain, healed poisoned food, ate angel's food, were fed by birds, and more.

Jesus is for the poor. However, He is more interested in developing their spirits than in always giving them money. The Lamb wants all the poor in spirit to control the spirit of their minds rather than allow their circumstances to control them. Thus, handouts to the poor should be done with understanding (Acts 3:6).

REMEMBERING THE POOR

*Galatians 2:10, NKJV: They desired only that we should **remember the poor**, the very thing which I also was eager to do.*

The apostles at Jerusalem wanted Paul to remember the poor, which he was eager to do. Thus, our walk with God requires us to give to the poor. The so called "giving chapters" (2 Corinthians, Chapters Eight and Nine) are, in reality, dedicated to the "poor among the saints who are in Jerusalem" (Romans 15:26, NKJV). Men use it more for getting money for themselves than for the poor. Yet remembering the poor is not always meant to provide for them in every way. This would continue the non-productive mode of their spirits. The Lord commanded the landowners to leave some of their produce for the poor (Acts 4:34-37).

The poor had to go get the portion the Lord left for them. I do understand that the poor will "never cease from the land." (Deuteronomy 15:11) I also understand that one of the purposes for the poor being on the earth; they are there to keep our hearts soft and our hands open to giving (Deuteronomy 15:7). Yet, those whose spirits are strong in the Lord must also do as Jesus did, empower the poor in spirit to rule in life by proper fathering in sonship.

We are required to do as the Lord do. He preached God's sonship dominion to them. He taught them to be productive. The gospel of the kingdom is not just focusing on "eating and drinking" (Romans 14:17). God is also interested in generating spirit-motivation to work in life. This is also seen in the fact that the poor in the Old Testament were also required to **go** get their "produce" that was left on the land for them.

Exodus 23:10-11, NKJV: [10]*Six years you shall sow your land and gather in its produce,* [11]*but the seventh year you shall let it rest and lie fallow, that the poor of your people may eat;* **and what they leave,** *the beasts of the field may eat. In like manner you shall do with your vineyard and your olive grove.*

The Scriptures indicated that the poor had to go get their produce by the fact the landowners had the choice to **"leave"** some behind. As a young boy in Jamaica West Indies, I learned a principle that I remember to this day. A man asked my father for fifty cents. (My father was building a school at the time, and we were at the site that day.) My father's response impacted me. Allow me to relay the event.

There was a discarded car tire on the construction site. He told the man to go get the tire and take it to a gas station (which was a little way off from the school) and for the man to return it for the fifty cents. The man did it and came back for the money. At a young age, I observed the event and received instruction.

The instruction was that a person has to work in order to receive money. My father did not give him the money for free. My father was also showing the man a principle. The man had to learn to work in order to get money. In fact, the giver had worked for the money that he was able to give to the beggar. Again, I am not saying, do not give to the poor. I am not saying to be rude and insensitive. On the contrary, I am saying help the poor by also developing their crouching spirits to be standing spirits.

Let us be like the Lamb and "bless" them with "length" of spirit in place of the short spirit. This can be accomplished by love and support. Let us not keep the poor in a state of neediness by not teaching them how to dominate.

With that said, I also understand that some of the poor will choose to be poor. However, let us continue to "bless" them with the opportunity to have a "large" spiritual capacity in lieu of a non-productive spirit. The gospel of the kingdom of God being **"at hand"** is the key

KINGDOM OF GOD AT HAND

Mark 1:14-15, NKJV: [14]*... Jesus came ... preaching **the gospel** of the kingdom of God,* [15]*and saying, "**The time is fulfilled, and the kingdom of God is at hand.***

The truth that the Lamb of God declared the kingdom of God to be "at hand" is significant to the poor Saints and to all Saints. Short, spirited people are very impatient. They need intervals of speedy results to encourage them to continue to grow in spirit.

This is why they need to know that the King's dominion is not far away in space somewhere. It is squeezing us like a throttle. The poor in spirit have to understand this truth. The Lord is at hand to fulfill His desire to see their spirit prosper in dominion. One of the lies that plague the poor is that poverty is their permanent lot. Some also believe that no one is available to aid them to overcome the state they are in. This is not true relative to the Lamb of God. He came preaching the gospel to the poor.

He promised the "King's domain" to them — **"Blessed** are the **poor in spirit,** for theirs is the **kingdom** of **heaven."** (Matthew 5:3). Luke 6:20, says it this way: "Blessed are you **poor**, for yours is the **kingdom** of **God**." Through the Lamb's sacrifice we can now rule in life again, as it was before Adam forfeited his dominion. Men and women's spirits were created in God's image to dominate. The poor can dominate again through Jesus. These are the days when the poor will realize speedy results through the dominion of the Lord. Jesus is Lord of all things. Jesus' Spirit is indomitable!

THE THRONE OF THE LAMB

Revelation 22:1-3, NKJV: ¹*And he showed me* ***a pure river of water of life,*** *clear as crystal, proceeding from the* ***throne*** *of God and* ***of the Lamb.*** ²*In the middle of its street, and on either side of the river, was the tree of life, which bore twelve fruits, each tree yielding its fruit every month. The leaves of the tree were for the healing of the nations.* ³*And there shall be* ***no more curse,*** *but the throne of God and of the Lamb shall be in it, and His servants shall serve Him.*

There are many concepts about the throne of the Lamb. Most think of His throne with Him being a ruler over Men. This is true but not complete. However, from the throne of the Lamb—the place of Ruling—there is "a pure river of water...proceeding." Because of the Lamb's throne, "there shall be no more curse ...." The true throne of the Lamb brings pure water. The true throne of the Lamb brings life. The true throne of the Lamb brings a pure river. The true throne of Lamb nullifies curses.

NO MORE CURSE

Revelation 22:1-3, NKJV: And there shall be no ***more curse,*** *but the throne of God and of the Lamb shall be in it, and His servants shall serve Him.*

In the verses above we see that the Lamb's throne replaces all curses. The word used for "curse" in the King James Version is a compound of three words—"kata" (down); "ana" (up, again, but) and "tithemi" (to put or place). This can be understood as sometimes a person may "place" himself/herself "up" with God as in "serving" God. Sometimes a person may "put down" himself/herself as in not "serving" God.

The Alexandrian text and Majority texts (Byzantine texts) uses a compound of two words for the word "curse." Those manuscripts use the words "kata" (down) and "tithemi" (down)—to place down, or to put down Therefore a curse or to curse someone means to "put down" a person. Thus, a curse can be the inability to serve God and the Lamb in a stable manner. The Lamb's throne is stable and uplifting. The presence of the Lamb's throne in New Jerusalem causes His servants to "serve" Him.

A curse may still be in operation when we are up one minute with the Lamb—we serve Him; and then we are down the next minute—we cannot find the strength to serve the Lamb. What the Church must know is that there are no more curses. Instability in serving the Lord has been vanquished.

Galatians 3:13-14, NKJV: [13] **Christ has redeemed us from the curse of the law**, *having become a curse for us (for it is written, "Cursed is everyone who hangs on a tree"),* [14] *that the* **blessing** *of Abraham might come upon the Gentiles in Christ Jesus, that we might receive the promise of the Spirit through faith.*

Christ the Lamb has already redeemed us from "the ...curse...." We do not have to be unstable in serving Him. His Blood rules our former up-and-down nature. We are on a plane of constancy in Him through the Lamb's throne. We are blessed with the same blessing of Abraham! Abraham did not "waver" at the promises of God (Romans 4:20).

2 Corinthians 1:19-20, NKJV: [19]*For the Son of God, Jesus Christ, who was preached among you by us – by me, Silvanus, and Timothy – was not Yes and No, but in Him was Yes.* [20] *For all the promises of God in Him are Yes, and in Him Amen, to the glory of God through us.*

We are no longer cursed, being "placed up" and "put down" like a yo-yo. We say yes one minute and the next minute we say no. We feel like God loves us one minute and the next minute we feel like he hates us — these things ought not to be.

The Lamb loves us unconditionally. In the Lamb, the promises are always Yes and Amen, not yes and no. There is no instability in Him. We can serve the living God in constancy. The dead works of instability have been removed by the Lamb's blood.

Hebrews 9:14, NKJV: How much more shall the blood of Christ, who through the eternal **Spirit** *offered Himself without spot to God, cleanse your* **conscience** *from dead works to* **serve** *the living God?*

The Blood of the Lamb purges our conscience from dead works. He enables us through His Blood to "serve the living God." Therefore, the Lamb's throne, through His blood, purges the heart of the curse conscious person.

The practical sign that the blood of the Lamb is at work is our ability to "serve" God and the Lamb. In other words, the very fact that you are serving the Lamb means that the curse is reversed. That is what Hebrews 9:14 above is saying. The throne (rule) of the Lamb of God **is** in your life. God wants you to serve Him by understanding that He does not criticize.

James 1:5, NIV: If any of you lacks wisdom, he should ask God, who gives generously to all **without finding fault,** *and it will be given to him.*

The Lord is not a faultfinder. He is not criticizing His people. He doesn't find fault in you one minute and then the next minute criticize you. The curse of being up and down is no more. The Lamb has redeemed us from all curses. If we are still being conscious of good and evil, we have not appropriated the throne of the Lamb. The Lamb's blood has purged us from a consciousness of evil.

Men of God should be primarily teaching His righteousness, not necessarily citing our evil doings. I am not saying that we should not correct the Saints. What I am saying is we should not smite the elevated rock (Christ and His Body) a second time (this was the mistake of Moses).

We should speak to the elevated rock the second time. We should speak that the blood of the Lamb, the smitten Rock, has freed us from being smitten a second time by men's doctrines. Our consciousness should not be evil, but the good work of the Lamb.

Hebrews 10:22-23, NKJV: Let us draw near with a true heart in full assurance of faith, having our hearts **sprinkled**[15] *from an* **evil conscience (or a consciousness of evil)** *and our bodies washed with pure water.*

The Church is too conscious of curses. We do not have to be conscious of evil. Our consciousness should be under the rule of the Lamb's Blood. We should not be conscious of "works" that are "dead" — dead works. The dead work of curses are purged by the blood of the Lamb and enforced by the Lamb's throne. The presence of the Lamb's throne in us (New Jerusalem) causes us to "serve" God and the Lamb. This is the blessing. The curse was replaced with the throne of the Lamb.

Revelation 22:3, NKJV: And there shall be no more curse, **but** *the throne of God and of the Lamb shall be in it, and His servants shall serve Him.*

The Lamb's throne is in us **instead** of a curse—"…no more curse, **but** the throne…of the Lamb. There is no more instability. The throne of man (wavering) is replaced with the faithful throne of the Lamb (purity). New Jerusalem, the Church, the Lamb's wife is the

---

[15] Sprinkled by Jesus' blood (Hebrews 12:24)

place of His throne. In this place is stability to serve Him. This is significant relative to the "pure river of water of life."

PURE RIVER OF WATER OF LIFE

*Revelation 22:1, NKJV: And he showed me **a pure river of water of life, clear (lit.; radiant, lamp or lamp)** as crystal, proceeding from the **throne** of God and **of the Lamb**.*

We serve God and the Lamb in stability by allowing the constant flow of the river, the flow of the water, and the flow of the life. The curse interrupts but the Lamb's throne causes a constant flow of the river. This river is also **"clear** as crystal," **"clear"** being defined from the Greek as shining, a **torch** or a **lamp**.

Thus, the pure river is linked to the "seven torches" which are the Seven Spirits of God (Revelation 4:5). They flow from the throne of the Lamb as the Spirit of Life. The Lamb's throne is ruling in your life when the gifts and the fruit of the Holy Spirit flow from you purely. The Lamb's throne is ruling in your life when the "lamp" as crystal is seen in you.

Have you ever heard this: a river that is also a lamp? This can only happen in the Spirit of God. As stated earlier, the word "clear" is from the same root of the "Seven Lamps of fire" which are the Seven Spirits of God (Revelation 4:5). Thus, this river of water of life also is a **"lamp"** to the place where it flows. This is the same as being filled with the Spirit and flowing in the gifts of the Holy Spirit. One of the ways the river flows is by praying in the Spirit. In other words, when we the Spirit manifest the gifts and fruit of the Holy Spirit through the corporate Christ, Jesus' Body, the river is being released to be a lamp, health, life, direction, wisdom, and so on.

John 7:37-39, NKJV: ³⁷*On the last day, that great day of the feast, Jesus stood and cried out, saying, "If anyone thirsts, let him come to Me and drink.* ³⁸*He who believes in Me, as the Scripture has said, out of his heart will flow* **rivers of living water."** ³⁹*But* **this He spoke concerning the Spirit,** *whom those believing in Him would receive; for the* **Holy Spirit was not yet given,** *because Jesus was not yet glorified.*

The "river of **living** water" is the same as the "river of water of life." The life-giving river is the Holy Spirit as indicated above. The called-out one is New Jerusalem that releases the life giving **Holy (lit.; Pure) Spirit**—the "pure" river of water. The practical application of this is praying in the Holy Spirit, the speaking of the water of the Word of God, speaking in tongues, functioning in Holy Spirit power, manifesting the word of wisdom, or the word of knowing, pilotage, and so on. With that said, as an example, Paul calls praying in the spirit the same as praying in tongues. The river is the Pure Spirit according to Jesus and the apostle John.

1 Corinthians 14:14-15, NKJV: ¹⁴*For if I pray in a tongue, my* **spirit** *prays…*¹⁵*What is the conclusion then?* **I will pray with the spirit,** *and I will also pray with the understanding.* **I will sing with the spirit,** *and I will also sing with the understanding.*

Praying in tongues is praying in the Pure Spirit. Praying in the Spirit with the spirit should be a constant thing. Paul says, "I thank my God 1 speak with tongues **more** than you all" (1 Corinthians 14:18, NKJV). Paul spoke in tongues "more" as in "constant." Jude also said that we are to pray in the Holy Spirit building up or most holy faith (Jude 1:20). This prayer in the Spirit of God helps to establish the rule of God in and through His people.

The rule of the Lamb's throne must be allowed. From His throne flows the Pure River of the Water of Life. The purposes of the river of water of life flowing is to bring life and cause the tree(s) of life to bear the fruit of the Spirit.

PURE WATER FOR THE TREES OF LIFE

Revelation 22:1-2, NKJV: ¹*And he showed me **a pure river of water of life,** clear as crystal, proceeding from the **throne** of God and **of the Lamb**... and on **either side of the river,** was the tree of life, which bore twelve fruits, each tree yielding its fruit every month. The leaves of the tree were for the healing of the nations.*

From the throne of the Lamb flows the river of life. On either side of the river was the tree of life. The river brought nourishment (life) to the tree of life. This tree was on both ("either") sides of the river. The nourishment causes the trees to produce fruit every month. Ezekiel saw this same truth concerning the temple (Ezekiel 47:1). Water flowed from the right side of the temple which watered "all kinds of trees."

*Ezekiel 47:12, NKJV: Along the bank of the river, on this side and that, will grow **all kinds of trees** used for food; their leaves will not wither, and their fruit will not fail. They will bear fruit every month because their water flows from the sanctuary. Their fruit will be for food, and their leaves for medicine.*

Did you hear that? The fruit of the trees of life (the "man" Jesus of Psalms 1) did not "fail." There is no failure in the fruit of those who allow the river to flow. Those who allow "failure" in fruit bearing are exemplified by the fact that one month they bear fruit, and then the next month they may not bear fruit.

The tree of life through the Life Giving Pure Spirit "bears fruit **every** month." There is no curse. Why do they bear fruit? "Because their water flows from the sanctuary" (the Church of the Living God).

The Water of the Pure Spirit must flow from us. Thus, it begs the questions. Why is the fruit of the Spirit not constant in our lives?

We are not praying in the Holy Spirit with our spirit enough. According to Paul and Jude, praying with spirit or praying in the Spirit "builds" you up. The "water" must flow from the throne of the Lamb who is in His holy temple, the Church.

We are the sanctuary (temple) of God (1 Corinthians 6:19). The purpose of this water of the Holy Spirit is to cause us to bear the fruit of the Spirit in our lives. For example, speaking in tongues (a form of the Water of the Spirit flowing to humanity) cause the nations to hear the **"wonderful works of God"** (Acts 2:11). You are a tree of life, just like Jesus; and it is the River of Life that causes us the bear fruit. This comes as we delight in the **Law** of the Spirit of Life offered by the Lamb of God (Romans 8: 2).

*Psalms1:1-3, NKJV: ¹Blessed is the man who walks not in the counsel of the ungodly, nor stands in the path of sinners, nor sits in the seat of the scornful; ²But his delight is in the **law** of the LORD, and in His law, he meditates day and night. ³**He shall be like a tree** planted **by the rivers of water that brings forth its fruit in its season,** whose leaf also shall not wither; and whatever he does shall prosper.*

A man who delights in the Law of God—the Law of the Spirit of Life (Romans 8:2) and meditates in His Law is like a tree. This Man foremost is Jesus (John 4:29). This man is also those who become like "the Man" (Ephesians 4:13). Thus, there is **the** Tree of Life, Jesus; and there are trees of life (the Saints of the Living God).

According to the Psalm, being planted by the "rivers of water" causes the tree to bear "fruit in its season." There is some fruit that the Lamb wants His Church to bear in a set season. However, if the Church does not water their tree by the gifts and fruit of Holy Spirit, regularly, the fruit may wither. The wonderful works of God may not be heard as they ought.

Yet, thanks be to God, because from the Lamb's throne flows this water of life. This means that even when we do not pray, He prays for us through His Pure Spirit. His purpose is to "affect" us on the "inside," to cause us to pray in the Spirit also. His purpose is to help us with our weaknesses. His purpose is to help us eventually to bear pleasant fruits.

Romans 8:26-27, NKJV: ²⁶Likewise the Spirit also helps in our weaknesses. For we do not know what we should pray for as we ought, but **the Spirit Himself makes intercession for us with groanings which cannot be uttered.** *²⁷Now He who searches the hearts knows what the mind of the Spirit is, because* **He makes intercession** *for the saints according to the will of God.*

"Intersession" as defined from the Greek is a compound of three words: "over," "in" and "affect." The Pure Spirit is "over" us and is praying "in" us to "affect" us on the inside. Can you see this? His **inter-cession is affecting** us on the **inside.** He "helps" us in our weakness of not being constant in prayer.

He does this by groaning which cannot be uttered. He is causing the river of life to affect us on the inside when we are weak. In other words, He causes the river to flow through intercession, as the Spirit groans in us, even though we may be feeling weak. Again, The Spirit causes the river of His life to flow in us even with words that cannot be articulated.

We call it "groaning." This is the ability of the rule of the Lamb's throne. He extends His rule by the ancient river of the Holy Spirit. He extends His "help" through the intercession of the Spirit.

A person is incomplete without the Pure Spirit. As indicated earlier, the Pure Spirit is that river of water of life that causes the trees (us) to bear fruit. He is the one who waters your life to bear fruit. The fruit is for food and the leaves are for healing. Praying in the Spirit with the spirit helps the healing process. That is, our faith is built up by praying in the Spirit. Thus, our edified faith that heals through love can flow freely.

FRUIT FOR FOOD, LEAVES FOR HEALING

Revelation 22:1-2, NKJV: ¹*And he showed me **a pure river of water of life,** clear as crystal, proceeding from the **throne** of God and **of the Lamb**... was the tree of life, which bore twelve fruits, each tree yielding its fruit every month. The leaves of the tree were for the healing of the nations.*

*Ezekiel 47:12, NKJV: ...They will **bear fruit**[16] every month, **because** their water flows from the sanctuary. Their fruit will be for food, and their leaves for medicine.*

At "the scent of water" a stump of a tree will "bud" (Job 14:9). Therefore, at just the scent of the river of life the trees will bud. By the flow of the River of the Spirit of Life, the fruits are produced. These fruits are for food. Foremost, the fruits of the trees are for the Lamb. Second, they are for the nations who do not know God.

*Song of Solomon 4:16, NKJV: ...Let my **beloved** come to **his** garden and eat its pleasant **fruits**.*

The Beloved is Jesus, the Lamb of God. The garden is the Church. The "pleasant fruits" are for Him to "eat." We are required to bear fruit to feed God. Our lives should be a "pleasant" place for the Lamb of God. It follows that the river of the water of life from the throne of the Lamb causes us to produce pleasant fruits. The lambkins should be a very pleasant people, even in the face of

---

[16] Lit., firstborn fruit, birthright fruit, and so on

being killed for your belief in the Lord. Remember Stephen in Acts 7:60.

One of the purposes of the river of the water of life is to produce pleasant fruit[17] every month. We should be praying regularly in the Spirit so that every month we produce a fruit. In the words of Ezekiel, "They will bear fruit every month, **because** their water flows from the sanctuary." In the words of the beloved John, "each tree **yielding (lit.; to give away)** its fruit every month" is made to bud by the river of life.

We should have such "pleasant fruit" we will be able to "give them away." You know you have pleasant fruit when people say, "it is so refreshing to be around you." Or "you are so pleasant and sweet." The fruit produced by the Pure Spirit is pleasant and sweet.

The fruit of the Spirit of **Love** is sweet and pleasant. The fruit of the Spirit of **Joy** is sweet and pleasant. The fruit of the Spirit of **Peace** is sweet and pleasant. The fruit of the Spirit of **Longsuffering** is sweet and pleasant. The fruit of the Spirit of **Kindness** is sweet and pleasant. The fruit of the Spirit of **Goodness** is sweet and pleasant. The fruit of the Spirit of **Faithfulness** is sweet and pleasant.

The fruit of the Spirit of **Gentleness** is sweet and pleasant. The fruit of the Spirit of **Self-control** is sweet and pleasant. The fruit of the Spirit of **Righteousness** is sweet and pleasant. The fruit of the Spirit of **Truth** is sweet and pleasant. The fruit of the Spirit of our **lips giving thanks to His name** is sweet and pleasant. The fruit of **Spiritual gifts that establish the Saints** is sweet and pleasant. The

---

[17] The "fruit" that the Tree of Life produces every month is foremost Jesus, the firstborn who has the birthright (see Ezekiel 47).

fruit of the Spirit is **"good" (honest)** (Galatians 5:22-23; James 3:18; Ephesians 5:9, Hebrews 13:15; Romans 1:10-13, Matthew 7:18).

These are among the fruits that the River of life bears on the trees. Yes! There are more than twelve listed above. That is because twelve is a symbol of the Day's (Jesus') apostolic government. In other words, these are the fruit of the Spirit that exemplify the Lamb of God; and there are more than twelve.

Our job is to allow our trees to yield their fruit and then give them away to those who need to eat from your fruitful life. The same is also true for the leaves. They are for the healing of the nations. Nations are sick and hurting. We have a responsibility to heal them through the Tree of Life and the trees of life.

*Revelation 22:2, NKJV: ... The **leaves** of the tree were for the **healing** of the nations.*

"Leaves," according to its etymology, also mean "tribes." The Church is made up of twelve tribes. Every Believer is of a designated tribe. The nations were divided into twelve tribes.

*Deuteronomy 32:8, NKJV: When the Most High **divided their inheritance to the nations,** when He separated the sons of Adam, He set the boundaries of the peoples **According** to the **number** of the children of Israel.*

How many sons did Israel have? The answer is twelve. God "divided the nations...According to the **number [12] children of Israel.**" In every nation there are twelve tribes. Africa is tribal; Europe is tribal. Mexico is tribal, Asia is tribal, and South America is tribal. The same is true for the Church which is made up of all nations. Each of the twelve tribes (leaves) is required to bring healing to the nations.

Therefore, the tribe of Jesus, which is Judah (Worship), is a healer. The tribe of Asher (Joy) is a healer. The tribe of Dan (Judge) is a healer, and so on. The healing is **therapeutic** for so is the transliteration of the Greek word for healing. The tribes must **serve as an attendant** for the nations. This **service** does not mean what you think. This service as an attendant means to deliver the nations.

Hebrews 3:5, NKJV: And Moses indeed was faithful in all His house as a **servant (lit.; therapist)**, *for a testimony of those things which would be spoken afterward.*

The service of the leaves (tribes) is that of a deliverance ministry like Moses.' Except this time, all the tribes of the Lamb will be involved; and the deliverance will be the deliverance of the **nations**. The same Spirit that was on Moses and in Moses will once again flow through the Church. The Church of the Lamb will send forth her tribes in the Spirit and Power of Moses.

The Spirit and Power of Moses is the Holy Spirit of God. We are to "heal" the nations by "serving" the nations through the "ways" and "acts" of the Lamb. The lambkins must begin to think nationally. We are called to shepherd the nations with the Lamb, now!

Revelation 2:26-27, NKJV: [26]*And he who overcomes, and keeps My works until the end, to him I will give* **power over** *the* **nations** *–* [27]*'He shall* **rule (lit.; shepherd, pastor)** *them with a rod of iron; they shall be dashed to pieces like the potter's vessels' – as I also have received from My Father.*

I quoted the verses above to show that as we "overcome," the Lamb will give us "lawful right" over the nations. The Overcomers will "shepherd" the nations. The goal of the great commission as it is known is national and international. We must teach and disciple the nations. The Church must cease from trying to leave the earth, and the nations have not become disciples as of yet.

Matthew 28:19-20, NKJV: *¹⁹Go therefore and make **disciples** of **all the nations**, baptizing them in the name of the Father and of the Son and of the Holy Spirit, ²⁰**teaching them** to observe **all things** that I have commanded you; and lo, I am with you always, even to the end of the age." Amen.*

The nations have not been taught "all things" that the Church knows about the Lamb. The Church with the Tree of Life in the middle of her and her several trees must allow the nations to eat her leaves for "medicine" according to Ezekiel. The Church must be that therapist that delivers the nations by teachings and making disciples of nations. We are not done yet! We cannot leave just yet. There is work to be done. The nations must be healed.

The water of the river of life is causing the trees of life to produce and give away their fruits. The leaves of the Church are also medicinal for the nations. Our heart must be "merry" about the prospect of the nations being healed.

This "merriness" of heart is like a medicine (Proverbs 17:22). Saying it another way; as we cause the nations to be "merry" in the Lamb's finished work, their hearts will be healed through that medicine of merriness. Amen!

THE LAMB'S WIFE

Revelation 21:2, NKJV: Then I, John, saw **the holy city, New Jerusalem, coming down** *out of heaven from God, prepared as a* **bride** *adorned for her* **husband.**

Revelation 21:9-10, NKJV: ⁹Then one of the seven angels who had the seven bowls filled with the seven last plagues came to me and talked with me, saying, **"Come, I will show you the bride, the Lamb's wife."** *¹⁰And he carried me away in the Spirit to a great and high mountain, and showed me the great[18] city, the* **holy Jerusalem**, *descending out of heaven from God*

*Ephesians 5:31-32, NKJV: ³¹"For this reason a man shall leave his father and mother and be joined to his wife, and the two shall become one flesh." ³²***This is a great mystery,** *but I speak concerning* **Christ** *and* **the church.**

The Lamb's wife is New Jerusalem, which the apostle Paul named as the Church. There are some differences concerning who the Lamb's wife really is. This is due to the fact that some see New Jerusalem as a mystical city in space somewhere. This is far from the truth.

I have learned over the years that the Bible is remarkably simple when the Holy Spirit teaches us how to understand spiritual things. **One of the first principles of studying the Scriptures is:**

---

[18] The word "great" is omitted by the Majority Greek Texts (M) and the Alexandrian Test (NU). Therefore, "great" is not in the original Greek Texts. See NASU, NIV, TLB, RSV, NAS. I noted this truth because it is significant relative to the study of "Mystery Babylon."

what do the Scriptures say? That may seem too simple for some. However, that is the easiest way to study the Scriptures.

The Scriptures say that the Lamb's wife is New Jerusalem. Paul picks this up by calling the Lamb's wife the Church. Thus, New Jerusalem is the Church. It is that simple in one sense. Yet, the Bible calls this a "great mystery." One of the reasons why this is a great mystery is: how can a City be a Wife or Woman? The truth is New Jerusalem is a living entity. I will prove this point with another "city" that is also called a "woman."

THE CITY OF BABYLON, A WOMAN

*Revelation 17:1-3, NKJV: Then one of the seven angels who had the seven bowls came and talked with me, saying to me, "Come, I will show you the judgment of the great harlot who sits on many waters... So, he carried me away in the Spirit into the wilderness. And I saw a **woman**....*

*Revelation 17:18, NKJV: And the **woman** whom you saw is that great **city** which reigns over the kings of the earth."*

Babylon, a "woman," is called a "city." That is what the Scripture above states. That is the understanding of this entity via Scripture interpreting Scripture. Now, if the woman, Babylon is called a city, why is it so difficult for some to acknowledge that New Jerusalem is the Woman (Wife) of Christ? It is logical to me that a city can be called a woman.

The Lamb's Wife is the City New Jerusalem, and she is not in space somewhere. She is right here on the earth, as well as in heaven (Ephesians 2:6 w/John 3:13). She may not be totally filled with the glory of God; however, she is right here on earth. Her full **descent** (birth) may not be unveiled, yet her buildings (us) can be seen. The Lamb's wife is the Church of the Living God. Most get stuck on the fact that New Jerusalem is "coming down out of heaven from God;" therefore, She cannot be the Church.

NEW JERUSALEM'S DESCENT

Revelation 21:2, NKJV: Then I, John, saw the holy city, New Jerusalem, **coming down** *out of heaven from God, prepared as a* **bride** *adorned for her husband.*

What does it mean to come down from heaven? This can be found in the mind of Christ, meaning God's thinking is always opposite ours. Men are looking for some city to fall out of the sky. God sees it differently. He sees New Jerusalem coming down from heaven **(new heaven)** through the means of birth.

John 3:13, NKJV: No one has ascended to heaven but **He who came down from heaven,** *that is, the Son of Man who is in heaven.*

Remember I stated earlier that the first step to understanding the Bible is to ask yourself what does the Scripture say? Therefore, I pose this question. **How did the Lamb of God come down from heaven?** The Lamb of God was **birthed** through Mary after conception through the Holy Spirit. Thus, the avenue by which the Lamb "came down" from heaven was through the birth canal of a woman as a result of a conception of the Holy Spirit.

The same is true for New Jerusalem. The Lamb's wife is descending from heaven through the birthing process. The womb of a woman is a portal of heaven. Heaven's people are brought down to earth through the portal of a woman. That is why sexuality, natural and spiritual, must be pure.

The same is true for other spiritual things. The things of the Spirit descend from heaven as the Church births it through prayer. The

Lamb's wife descends into the natural as the Church births her from the invisible to the visible through the travail of prayer.

"This is a great mystery...concerning Christ and His Church." Paul was part of the Church, yet this same Paul was **as** a mother in the Church. He travailed in birth pangs until Christ was formed in the believers. This mystery is great, yet it can be understood.

Galatians 4:19, NKJV: My little children, for whom I **labor in birth** *again until Christ is formed in you.*

Paul was part of the Church; and he was birthing a heavenly entity in the people of God through prayer. The glory of the Lamb's wife will be seen as the Church births her in prayer. The Lamb's bride is descending through the heavenly portal of the womb of the people of God. Can you see this?

New Jerusalem exists in the heavenly realm; and she is seen in the visible realm through the birthing of prayer. The Lamb always existed. However, His manifestation in the earth was through the womb of the Virgin Mary. The Lamb of God left His Father, and He came down to the earth through the portal of the birth canal. New Jerusalem will be unveiled in a similar manner.

One of the Lamb's objectives is to marry His Bride and consummate the union. This is another part of this great mystery. He left the Father; He also had to leave His mother to perform His duties as a Husband. The New Jerusalem is married spiritually, and it shall also be manifest in the visible.

LEAVING MOTHER AND FATHER

Ephesians 5:31-32, NKJV: [31]*"For this reason a man shall* **leave** *his father and mother and be joined to his wife, and the two shall become one flesh."*

*³²This is a great mystery, but I speak concerning **Christic** and **the church**.*

The Lamb left His Mother at the cross. He left His Mother and assigned His beloved disciple to take her in. As for His father "by law," the Bible does not mention Joseph after age twelve of Jesus. Jesus also left His Father in heaven to come and die for His wife the Church. Thus, the phrase in Ephesians above is a current reality.

*John 19:25-27, NKJV: ²⁵Now there stood by the cross of Jesus His mother, and His mother's sister, Mary the wife of Clopas, and Mary Magdalene. ²⁶When Jesus therefore saw His mother, and the disciple whom He loved standing by, **He said to His mother, "Woman, behold your son!" ²⁷Then He said to the disciple, "Behold your mother!"** And from that hour that disciple took her to his own home.*

Paul states that the marriage of the Lamb **"is"** a great mystery (Ephesians 5:32). The word "is" is "present tense" in Ephesians 5:21. As seen above, Jesus indicated to Hs mother at the cross that He was leaving her to another son. Why? He was about to be joined to His Bride. Therefore, the marriage is a present experience. Yet, His Wife is also being prepared for presentation to Him as a glorious Church.

JERUSALEM HAVING THE GLORY OF GOD

Revelation 21:10-12, NKJV: ¹⁰And he carried me away in the Spirit to a great and high mountain, and showed me the great city, the holy

Jerusalem, descending out of heaven from God, ¹¹*having* **the glory of God**[19]....

Ephesians 5:25-27, NKJV: ²⁵*Husbands, love your wives, just as Christ also loved the church and gave Himself for her,* ²⁶*that He might sanctify and cleanse her with the washing of water by the word,* ²⁷*that He might* **present** *her to Himself a* **glorious** *church, not having spot or wrinkle or any such thing, but that she should be holy and without blemish.*

2 Corinthians 11:2, NKJV: ...I have **betrothed** *you to* **one husband** *that I may* **present** *you as a chaste virgin to Christ.*

What is the glory of God? There are many definitions. One can look at the Greek definition. One can also look at the English definition. However, the Biblical definition may best exemplify the glory of God which became the glory of the Church.

Romans 3:23, NKJV: For all have **sinned** *and* **fall short** *of the* **glory** *of God.*

The Bible defines itself. Sinning is falling short of God's glory. Therefore, not sinning is the glory of God. Saying it another way, God is absolutely sinless. Therefore, He has glory, and He is the glory. The Church will become "sin-free." Note, I did not say sinless like God. I said sin-free. There is a difference. **Jesus' blood "loosed"** us from our sins (Revelation 1:5, NU Text)

The Word of God says that if we say we do not have any sin, we are liars (1 John 1:8); thus, my statement of the Church becoming sin-free, not sinless. God's glory in New Jerusalem (the Church) is for her to be sin-free. Yes, we are free from sin.

---

[19] Note: Glory of God also represents resurrection power as Jesus demonstrated with Lazarus in John 11

As Paul stated, neither death nor sin can have dominion over us anymore because of the Lamb of God. Jesus is going to present His Wife to "Himself a glorious (sin-free) Church" There will be a time when the Church cannot sin. She is and will be full of glory.

*1 John 3:9, NKJV: Whoever has been born of God does not sin, for His seed remains in him; and **he cannot sin,** because he has been born of God.*

There is a birthing in God that will cause one not to sin. His seed remains in Him. "He cannot sin because he has been born of God." This is a Scripture that some Believers are afraid of because of sinning and according to the Scripture above, if one is truly "born **of (lit.; out of)** God" he/she **"cannot sin."** I want to help you. You can be born out of God more than once.

The resurrection is considered a "birthing" of God. I believe when this resurrection birthing, through travail, (Galatians 4:19) takes place in us, the Church "does not sin." The early Church is the seedbed — seminar — for the remaining Church through the ages.

There were some Believers in the early Church who experienced 1 John 3:9. They experienced the sin-free life. They walked in resurrection sonship; and note, children usually come after marriage. We are called to produce the Son in our lives (Galatians 4:19); therefore, let us put the marriage of the Lamb in perspective.

THE LAMB OF GOD RESURRECTED

*Acts 13:33, NKJV: God has fulfilled this for us their children, in that He has **raised up** Jesus. As it is also written in the second Psalm: 'You are My Son, today I have **begotten You.**'*

Paul walked in apostolic revelation. This great mystery was revealed to Paul. In the verse above, Paul called Jesus being "raised up" from the dead a "begotten." The resurrection of Jesus ("He has raised up Jesus") is the same **"As** it is written ... My Son, I have **begotten** You." Jesus was uniquely begotten out of God when Mary gave birth to Him (Luke 1:31-32). Jesus was "**begotten**" when he was resurrected (see Acts 13:33 above).

This is also true for the Church. The Believer is born again through faith at the beginning of his/her salvation. The believer will also experience a continual birthing (a becoming) into a sin-free lifestyle, knowing that they are indeed "loosed" from sins through Jesus' blood.

The Scripture says that "He [Jesus] will appear **out of** (the) **second**[20] apart from sin, into salvation" (see any Interlinear Greek structure). She will be glorious in her sin-free environment. She will become like her Husband experientially. She will be sin-free having the glory of God (Hebrews 4:15 w/1 John3:9). This is similar to her making herself internally fit to do righteous acts.

INTERNAL PREPARATION

*Revelation19:7-8, NKJV: [7]Let us be glad and rejoice and give Him glory, for the marriage of the Lamb **has come,** and His wife has made herself **ready**." [8]And to her it was granted to be arrayed in fine linen, clean and bright, for the **fine linen** is the **righteous acts** of the saints.*

The voice of the Scripture indicates that the marriage of the Lamb is taking place because she has made herself **ready**. **"Ready" is defined as internal fitness,** according to Strong's Concordance.

---

[20] The "second," according to the Scriptures, is the Holy of Holies ("behind the second veil"); or the second body (the body of Believers) (see the book of Hebrews).

This internal fitness is the ability to do righteous acts through the law of the Spirit of life in Christ Jesus.

*Romans 8:2-3, NKJV: ²For the **law of the Spirit of life** in Christ Jesus has made me **free** from the law of sin and death. ³For what the law could not do in that it was weak through the flesh, God did by sending His own Son in the likeness of sinful flesh, on account of sin: He condemned sin in the flesh, ⁴that the **righteous requirement** of the law might be **fulfilled (completed)** in us who do not walk according to the flesh but according to the Spirit.*

The Lamb showed us that it is possible to do "righteous acts" through the law of the Spirit of life. Jesus condemned sin in the flesh "that the righteous requirements of the law can be fulfilled (competed) **in us**...." This is the internal fitness that makes New Jerusalem ready for the marriage consummation. In the Spirit, the marriage, and the ability to do righteous acts already occurred. Yet, it must also be fulfilled experientially in the visible.

The nations should be able to look at us and see "fine linen," which is righteous acts. Saying it another way, nations should be able to look at us and see "glory" (Greek: doxa—a good opinion) of God." Did you know that the Scripture states that God's name is blasphemed because of the wrong things His people do.

New Jerusalem should be transparent—sin-free. She must "complete" the righteous acts of God, bodily. This is an internal issue. We must become fit internally. The emphasis on external fitness is not profitable for all things (1Timothy 4:8). The emphasis should be on internal fitness. Paul's concentration was not building buildings, physique building, or the like; his emphasis was to "present every man **perfect** in Christ" by **"warning" (lit.; to put in the mind).** The mind is internal. There is not enough emphasis on having internal character. According to the Bible, "the Vision" is a

"He" — Jesus. He is the Perfect One we should be characterizing, not temporal things.

*Colossians 1:28, NKJV: Him we preach, **warning** every man and teaching every man in all wisdom, that we may **present** every man **perfect** in Christ Jesus.*

*2 Corinthians 11:2, NKJV: For I am jealous for you with godly jealousy. For I have **betrothed** you to **one husband**, that I may **present** you as a **chaste (lit.; clean)** virgin to Christ.*

Paul was and still is concerned about the internal condition of Christ's Church. Cleanliness of virginity is what the Lamb is looking for in His bride. This is important to the Lamb. He marries a virgin. This virginity has to do with the mind. This is why Paul was constantly perfecting the saints by warnings, putting (the word of God) in the mind.

Some may say, I am defiled and no longer a virgin because of what I have done in the past, physically, and mentally. This can be corrected in the Lord. Let us look at a Biblical truth concerning natural marriages with regard to those who are not virgins and relative to God correcting or purifying the bed. We will then correlate that to the mind.

THROUGH MARRIAGE THE BED IS PURIFIED

Hebrews 13:4, NKJV: Marriage is honorable among all, and the bed undefiled ....

Marriage is "valuable" among all. Yes! There is value in marriage. The "bed" is also "undefiled." When does this occur? At marriage, the bed is made undefiled. In other words, at marriage if your bed was soiled, it becomes unsoiled through the blood of Jesus. To "undo" something is to make it like it was.

When we make a mistake on the computer and type something that we did not intend to type, we can use the "Undo" icon to erase the mistake. To "un" "defile" the bed is to make it like it used to be. "Bed" is defined in the Greek as the organ that receives the semen, sexual intercourse, the bed, the sex organ itself.

Thus, at marriage, the virginity of the bride and bridegroom is "un" defiled, if they were defiled before. The blood of the Lamb restores the purity of copulation, through marriage.[21] This is also true for those who may have defiled the Lamb's spiritual bed. He can "undo" the wrong deeds.

He can make you right again, mentally, and physically. This is done through the mind. Paul equates virginity to the mind. Thus, sexuality can be performed spiritually with false doctrines (through the mind) and physically. The virginity of the Church is the Church not allowing her mind to be defiled by other gospels, another spirit, and another Jesus.

*2 Corinthians 11:2-4, NKJV: ²For I am jealous for you with godly jealousy. For I have betrothed you to one husband, that I may present you as a **chaste virgin** to Christ. ³But I fear, lest somehow, as the **serpent deceived Eve** by his craftiness, **so your minds may be corrupted** from the simplicity that is in Christ. ⁴For if he who comes preaches **another** Jesus whom we have not preached, or if you receive a **different** spirit which you have not received, or a **different** gospel which you have not accepted — you may well put up with it!*

Above we see that Paul linked the "mind" to "virginity." Paul said, "I have betrothed you to one husband...**as a chaste virgin**...But I

---

[21] There is a couple who when they got married, the wife asked the Lord to restore her virginity (the hymen). The Lord obliged her; and when the marriage was consummated between the two, a covenant cut before the Lord.

fear your mind may be corrupted...." Thus, Eve broke her spiritual pureness (virginity) by allowing her "mind" to be infiltrated (corrupted) by a "different spirit," the tempter. This is true for all unbelievers. Their mental virginity or mental pureness is broken by the corruption of their mind. However, at the point of choosing to follow the Lamb in truth, they become **"as** ... virgin" all over again.

Proof: Paul called the Corinthians "virgins." This is significant considering their sexual background, spiritually and naturally. The Corinthians were idolaters, gay people, catamites, men-stealers, and incestuous. Yet, after they were rededicated to the Lamb, they were called "virgins." The book of Hebrews is true; marriage is valuable; and at marriage, any defilement is "un"-defiled by the marriage process. Isn't the Lamb awesome? That is why He and His ministers are so jealous over the Church. They do not want the Bride of the Lamb to lose her virginity all over again. She is presented to Him as internally fit. She is presented to Him as glorious. She is presented to Him **as** a pure virgin. The Church — New Jerusalem — is married to the Lamb of God.

THE LAMB'S FOOD

*John 4:32, NKJV: But He said to them, "I have **food** to eat of which you do not know."*

*1 Corinthians 6:13, NKJV: **Foods** for the **stomach** and the stomach for foods, but God will **destroy** both it and them. Now the **body** is not for sexual immorality but for the **Lord**, and the Lord for the body.*

The Holy Spirit teaches that food is for the stomach as the body is for the Lord. Or food is to the stomach as the body is to the Lord. Therefore, the function of "food" relative to the "stomach" is correlated to the function of the "body" relative to "the Lord."

Saying it another way: As the stomach holds food, so the body holds the Lord. The stomach uses food to nourish the body, as the body utilizes the Lord to nourish the human spirit and the human body. Therefore, the Lord is as important to the body as food is to the stomach.

Food is as materialistic as a person can get! We can live without lavish clothing. Growing up in Jamaica West Indies in the 1960s and 1970s, this was something I experienced to a degree; and I also saw among some. We can also live without sumptuous houses. Look at the so called undeveloped world (the Third World). We can even live without a car or a "horse and buggy." We were given feet. But food! That is a different story.

As stated before, food is as materialistic as one can get. According to the Scriptures, food has become so important to mankind that they will eat each other to survive a famine (2 Kings 6:24-30). Men even speak evil of God for scant food (Numbers 11). Men will even eat food with blood to satisfy their hunger (1 Samuel 14:32). My point: food is as materialistic as a person can get.

Yet, with the fact that food is so important, the Lord said He would "render inactive" both "food" and the "stomach" that was designed for food. The word translated as "destroy," in 1 Corinthians 6:13, means to render entirely inactive, to render useless, to render idle, to cease, to abolish, etc. (see Strong's Lexicon).

That means there is ability to live without "bread **alone**" (Matthew 4:4). I emphasize, I did not say that man can live without bread; I said man has the ability to live without bread, **alone**. Not living by "bread **alone**" means that there is **another** source of nourishment.

*John 4:32, NKJV: But He said to them, "I have **food** to eat of which you do not **know**."*

The Lamb of God did not need food as often as His disciples thought. He had another source of food that His disciple could not perceive at the time. Jesus was not dependent upon natural food. In fact, humans were designed to go forty days without food, as proven by Jesus; and Moses who went up to eighty days without food. That's right, eighty days!

There is a kind of food which can also sustain man as natural food can. This kind of food is not necessarily "seen." The Lamb's kind of food is that which could not be "known" (lit.; seen). Our eyes need to be opened to the Lord's food. When the body is totally nourished by the Lord (His Spirit), natural food is marginalized.

THE LORD IS FOR FOOD

1 Corinthians 6:13-17, NKJV: [13]***Foods** for the **stomach** and the stomach for foods, but God will **destroy** both it and them. Now the **body** is not for sexual immorality but for the **Lord**, and the **Lord for the body**…[17]But he who is joined to the Lord is one **spirit** with Him.*

The stomach (through stomach acid) breaks down food and releases the nourishment to the body through its wall. The Body does the same with the Lord through His Holy Spirit. When the "Body" is full of the Lord, the Body breaks down the spiritual nutrient from the Lamb and distributes it through the "Body." When this is realized to its fullest capacity, the "Body" then relies on the food of the Lamb; and marginalizes the food for the stomach.

There is a difference between your stomach growling for food and the body being hungry. Body hunger can be broken on a long fast; and pave the way for nourishment by the Lord. On a forty day fast, usually around the eighteenth (18th) to twenty-first (21st) day the **"body"** gets hungry, which is different from your stomach growling for food.

While on my first 40 days of fast, after a lesson from Dr. Myles Monroe and Kingsley Fletcher in 1992 on fasting, I experienced this "body hunger" as I call it. I must have tossed all night, even sweating, wanting to eat; yet I was not hunger. Because I remained steady and did not eat, the next morning the "body hunger" went away.

Thus, if discipline is maintained, the body can now have the opportunity to be nourished by the Lord by allowing your **body** to digest the "things of the Spirit of the Lord." The body can be nourished and trained not to always rely on "food alone." The Lord also nourishes the body as the stomach distributes nutrition through the stomach. The body will indeed need the strength of food, eventually.

The Word of God teaches that "princes" (leaders) should eat for "strength." However, natural "bread" should not be our only source of strength for the body. The Lamb said we should "…not live by **bread alone...**" (Matthew 4:4). There are other "kinds" of bread (food). This is the food that some cannot see. It is called doing the will (desire or pleasure) of God.

THE FOOD OF THE WILL OF GOD

*John 4:34, NKJV: Jesus said to them, "My **food** is to do the **will** of Him who sent Me, and to finish His work.*

This is what your natural body yearns for. The Lamb of God saw God's food and ate it. The Lamb's food was doing His Father's "will" (lit.; desire, pleasure). The Lamb understood that His "Body" needed to digest the "desire" of God more than any natural food. He conquered the force of natural food on His forty day fast. He rendered the stomach and the desire for food "useless."

In fact, according to Scripture, He also conquered death (rendered death inactive) when he overcame the "desire" for natural food on His forty days of fasting. He elevated Himself to a higher "desire" — the desire of His Father. The will of the Father is food; and in the context of when Jesus made His statement, the will of the Father is the work of the ministry.

The Lamb had just ministered prophetically to the woman at the well when the disciples thought He had already eaten natural food, after He refused to eat the food, they had brought back. The Lamb was filled with the bread of God, which is the will of God.

His mind was on the salvation of the whole city of Samaria that would happen through the woman at the well. We must find this same food for our lives — the will of the Father that will fill our bodies, and quiet our natural stomachs.

Food has become such a god to humanity that we obey it over God's will. The Church is being called to fast more often to demolish the "god of their belly." The Church is being urged on to know and do the "will" of the **only true** God.

THE GOD OF THE BELLY

Philippians 3:18-19, NKJV: [18]*For many walk, of whom I have told you often, and now tell you even weeping, that they are the **enemies of the cross of Christ:** [19]whose end is destruction, **whose god is their belly,** and whose glory is in their shame — who set their mind on earthly things.*

The verses cited above are interesting Scriptures. The belly can become a god. Belly denotes abdomen or womb. Thus, the god of one's "womb" can birth things (self-centeredness) that are "enemies of the cross of Christ." Or, the belly has become a god, in the sense of allowing "foods" to rule instead of doing the will of the Father.

These "foods" are also "enemies of the cross of Christ." The Scripture teaches that the land is curse when leaders eat for drunkenness rather than for strength. Following the god of one's belly can cause a person to get drunk with food.

*Ecclesiastes 10:17, NKJV: Blessed are you, O land, when your king is the son of nobles, and your princes **feast (lit.; eat)** at the proper time — for strength and not for **drunkenness**!*

The purpose of natural food is for strength. The meat of this is to be joined to the Lord so that food is only needed for strength. This is what the Lord found. The Lamb was so joined to God's will that God's will become His strength. The opposite is also important. Excessive eating of food can make a person drunk with food. This may be fresh to you. But food can make a person drunk, as too much alcohol can make a person drunk.

This means in the same manner drunkenness disables one's strength to control one's body, so drunkenness with food becomes a god to the body, instead of the Lord controlling the body. Ecclesiastes also gets a little stronger. Solomon states that the Leader who eats in the morning (breakfast) brings a "woe."

Ecclesiastes 10:16, NKJV: **Woe** *to you, O land, when your king is a child, and your princes* **feast (lit.; eat) in the morning!**

Now, I am not saying it is a sin to eat breakfast. The Resurrected Lord Jesus ate breakfast (John 21:3 w/21:12). The Scriptures state that breakfast should not become a feast. It should not become a god where we cannot give it up for fasting to do the Lord's will. The god of the belly is an enemy of the cross of Christ, according to Paul. The Church has become like the Cretans, "lazy" and "gluttons."

Titus 1:12, NKJV: One of them, a prophet of their own, said, "Cretans are always liars, evil beasts, **lazy gluttons.***"*

"Lazy gluttons" can also mean **"unemployed belly,"** barren belly, slow belly, inactive belly, barren womb. Their wombs were barren; the likeness of Jesus was not being birthed or formed in them. The Cretans were not working by fasting. Therefore, their [22]**bellies** ruled. Their own stomachs were their employment.

They worked to feed their bellies, rather than feeding their "body" with the will of God. We are striving to **"not live by bread alone,"**

---

[22] Note: this is not in referenced to size. I personally know men who are heavy and can fast forty days; and I also know men who are very skinny and struggle with their belly (desire to eat) after one or two days of fasting.

but by every **"word that proceeds from (or through) the mouth of God"** (Matthew 4:4).

For example, you may sit down to enjoy a nice meal; and a proceeding word from God's mouth may say, "Do not eat now, go and pray for the Third World." If a person is self-centered (his/her womb is ruling), they may override the will of the Spirit. If the belly is ruling, one may override that preceding word from God.

The belly begins to speak saying, "The sun is down, and it is time to eat." There are men of God who can only fast from sunup to sundown. In fact, they precede the sun, and eat before the sun comes up, then they fast, and as soon as the sun go down, the food is on the table.

Yes, it is okay at times to fast from sunup to sundown. However, we must constantly break the threshold of limitations if the Lord calls for a fast. I also understand that we should know our limitations. However, this does not license us to be lazy and only fast for a few hours here and there or ignore the voice of the Spirit.

Some of these men (not all) are lazy and they have not applied their bellies to fasting. The will of the Father is far from some of them. There is no power in their lives, even though they claim to be filled with power. Yet according to the Scripture, one of the ways the power (ability) of the Holy Spirit is released is after **proper**[23] fasting.

---

[23] Clothing the naked, feeding the poor, loosing bands of wickedness, and so on are also considered as proper fasting (see Isaiah 58).

POWER OF THE HOLY SPIRIT

Luke 4:1-2, NKJV: ¹*Then Jesus, being filled with the Holy Spirit, returned from the Jordan, and was led by the Spirit into the wilderness,* ²*being* **tempted for forty days** *by (lit.; under) the devil.* **And in those days, He ate nothing,** *and afterward when they had ended, He was hungry.*

The Lamb of God ate nothing for forty days. Since He is the pattern "man," the "last Adam," we can conclude that we are designed to go forty days without food. This is one of the keys for releasing the ability of the Spirit.

Luke 4:14-15, NKJV: ¹⁴*Then Jesus* **returned** *in the* **power (lit.; ability) of the Spirit** *to Galilee, and news of Him went out through all the surrounding region.* ¹⁵*And He taught in their synagogues, being glorified by all.*

Jesus "returned" in the "power" (Greek: "dunamis" (ability, force, and miracle)). Where did he return from? He returned from a forty day fast. He returned from being tempted "under" the devil. During the forty days of fasting, He was filled with the Holy Spirit. However, it was not until "after" the temptations and the fast, the ability of the Spirit began to work. Yes, when a person is filled with the Spirit, he/she have power (Acts 1:8).

However, the ability of power through the Spirit is fully released after testing and fasting (Luke 4:1 w/4:14). The Lord fasted for a reason during the trial. **Fasting was that which tempered His "body" in order not to be tempted by the tempter.** The Lamb tempered His stomach and body during the temptation. It was "afterward" (after the forty days); He was "hungry."

The Lamb returned in ability of the Spirit because He could be trusted. He controlled Himself by not using the Spirit to make food from stones. According to Scriptures, He conquered worldly pomp that comes through satanic worship; He overcame tempting God by not asking God to do something just to see if God can do it; and as indicated earlier, the Lamb also overcame food. He did not live by "bread alone."

Thus, the Father trusted Him with the creative ability of the Holy Spirit. Fasting is linked to ability. The first test was food because food is as materialistic as one can get. If He had fallen for food, the other two temptations would have been like a domino effect. This is partly what happened to Adam. Jesus is smart. He knew that controlling eating was a key to His Body releasing the ability of the Spirit.

The ability of the Spirit is not given to create food "alone." The ability of the Spirit is not given to get worldly pomp. The ability of the Spirit is not given to tempt God to do something for no apparent reason. The ability of the Spirit is for the healing of the nations, righteous acts, resurrection ability, casting out demons, righteous judgments, and so on.

The ability of the Spirit is not for abuse. However, this ability can be realized through the avenue of fasting and praying. Adam lost His authority and power through eating at the wrong time and the wrong fruit. However, the Lamb returning in the ability of the Spirit is linked to Jesus overcoming food, overcoming the world, and he not temping God. The will of God became His food, even in the wilderness.

Yes, the Lamb did not cry for "manna!" The Lamb did not ask for the glory of the kingdoms. He knew they already belonged to Him. He did not use His power to see if the angels would move on His behalf, just to see it happen. He then "returned" — lit.; turned under — the ability and authority of the Pure Spirit. The "desire" of the Father is the "desire" of the Lamb. As the Lamb Himself said,

"My **food** is to do the **will (lit.; desire)** of Him who sent Me, and to finish His work" (John 4:34, NKJV).

WHEN WE FAST

Matthew 6:16-18, NKJV: ¹⁶"*Moreover, **when you fast**, do not be like the hypocrites, with a sad countenance. For they disfigure their faces that they may appear to men to be fasting. Assuredly, I say to you, they have their reward. ¹⁷But you, when you fast, anoint your head and wash your face, ¹⁸so that you do not appear to men to be fasting, but to your Father who is in the secret place; and your Father who sees in secret will reward you openly.*

The Lamb indicated that we would have to ²⁴**fast**. He said, "When you fast…." He did not say, if you fast. He said, "When you fast…." Thus, we must fast at times. I had indicated earlier that we are designed to go forty days without food. This is just like a car that is designed to go 300 miles per hour. Because that car is designed to go 300 miles per hour, it can easily go 3 miles per hour.

The same is true for fasting; the body is designed to go forty days without food. Thus, fasting for three days should be "doable," and, in that same vein, fasting for forty days is not "absurd." Three (3) miles per hour is relatively easy for a car that can go 300 miles per hour. The same should be true for fasting. Three (3) days of fasting should be relatively easy compared to forty days of fasting.

---

²⁴ It is advisable for all who want to participate in fasting to discuss this issue with their Pastors and get a physical examination from a **competent** Doctor before fasting. My reference to fasting in this book is in no way mandating that a person fast. Anyone who decides to fast for any amount of time is solely responsible for his/her own choice to fast.

Now for those who may decide to fast forty days allow me to give you some pointers I learned a few years ago.[25] **(I also recommend rereading the footnote under this subheading "WHEN WE FAST")**. The habit of eating appears to be broken after the first three days. The first seven to fourteen days, the body begins the process of purging itself from impurity (This is evident in the discoloration of the urine). Days fourteen to twenty-one come to the breaking point.

If you can make it past days eighteen to twenty-one, you can make it to forty days. Days eighteen to twenty-one are when the body gets hungry. As I indicated earlier, this is different from stomach hunger. When the body gets hungry, some people break out in a cold sweat. A person may toss all night fighting the temptation to eat.

The "body's" hunger for food is a true test of the fast. And note: for some the hunger of the body begins at day fourteen. Once twenty-one days are past, the fast appears to be relatively easy. The body is then totally relying on the strength of the Lord. In fact, you begin to scare yourself by not having any desire to eat. However, do not panic. Right around the thirty-eighth day the stomach hunger comes back; and you will find yourself wanting to eat again.

During the fast, if a person plans to go forty-days, he/she should not work after day twenty-one. (On the first forty days fast that I completed, I did work for the first twenty one days as a drywall hanger and finisher). **One should also not get out of the bed suddenly when the fast reaches day thirty and so on!**

---

[25] Dr. Myles Monroe gave some of these points at a meeting in the early 90s.

For some, you have to be aware of this earlier than thirty days. A person has to know his/her own body. Water at room temperature should be drunk regularly. Nonacidic or low acidic juice can also be used.

Now, after the fast, do not eat heavy food immediately. One should gradually come off the fast. **Vegetable Soup,** cooked from scratch should be eaten. The food should be cooked long enough for the vegetables to be super-soft or mushy. Gradually increase the portion and the amount of times you eat per day. Food should be introduced to your body gradually. **Please be mindful that any person who decides to fast will be responsible for his/her own actions.**

THE LAMB'S WRATH

*Revelation 6:16, NKJV: And said to the mountains and rocks, "Fall on us and hide us from the face of Him who sits on the throne and from the **wrath** of the Lamb!*

The wrath of the Lamb is an interesting topic and there are many exegeses as to its meaning. However, before I define "wrath," via a Greek lexicon, let us look at the context of the wrath of the Lamb, as defined in the text above.

The first note is that people wanted to be "hid" and things were moved from the Lamb's wrath. They were not necessarily hiding from punishment. As it is, they were hiding from exposure. Part of the understanding of the wrath of the Lamb is that secret things were being exposed. In other words, the wrath of the Lamb was the uncovering of dark secrets. God was no longer "winking" at the idiocies of man (Acts 17:30, KJV).

THE SIXTH SEAL

*Revelation 6:12-17, NKJV: [12]I looked when He opened the sixth seal, and behold, there was a great earthquake; and the sun became **black as sackcloth of hair,** and the **moon became like blood.** [13] And the stars of heaven fell to the earth, as a fig tree drops its late figs when it is shaken by a mighty wind. [14] Then the sky **receded** as a scroll when it is rolled up, and every mountain and island was **moved (lit.; stirred to go)** out of its place. [15] And the kings of the earth, the great men, the rich men, the commanders, the mighty men, every slave, and every free man, **hid** themselves in the caves and in the rocks of the mountains, [16] and said to the mountains and rocks, "Fall on us and **hide** us from the **face of Him** who sits on the throne and from the **wrath of the Lamb!** [17] For the great day of His wrath has come, and who is able to stand?"*

Let us briefly look at how the sixth (6th) seal applies to this generation. The great earthquake can also mean "great gale." It points to the works of God independent of man's hands involved. The sun can point to the patriarch of a family, the moon is the matriarch of the family, and the stars are the children (see Genesis 37:9-10). The sun becoming **"black as sackcloth"** may reference the patriarchs in the Church who have been made **"dirty"** by living "bad" lives. Or it may point to the patriarchs in the Church who are morning to God with fasting, weeping and wailing.

"Black" is the Greek word "melas" from "mal" which properly means **"to be dirty."** A form of the word also means black ink. The Latin derivation from this word is "malus" which means **"bad."** **Sackcloth** points to "mourning" (Genesis 37:34). Sackcloth may point to "fasting, weeping and wailing" (Esther 4:3). Sackcloth also points to impoverish clothing (Isaiah 3:24).

Thus, the sun became "dirty as sackcloth of hair" may point to the patriarchs in the Church who are living a "bad" or "dirty" life. This badness caused their sunlight to be stained with dirt, like black ink stains. Thus, these "elders and leaders" were clothed with the dirty clothing of sackcloth of hair instead of "the rich or expensive clothing" of God's Sunlight (Jesus). In Isaiah 3:14-24, one of the of God's judgments upon the "elders and the leaders of the people" and Zion herself was that God clothed them with sackcloth instead of "fine clothing."

Another application is that God opened (unsealed) the fact that the leader in the Church (the sun) have become mourners with fasting, weeping, and tearing of the hair and beating of the chest in grief as the Asians do! This mourning may have resulted from the shock of God's great earthquake or great gale. Sackcloth is also a type of brokenness before the Lord. The great earthquake or gale may have brought the sun (patriarchs) to repentance.

The moon can be symbolic of the Church in general, who in spite of the "dirty" and "bad" leaders, still has **"life" (lit., soul)**. Leviticus teaches that the **life** of the flesh is in the blood. The Church is the flesh and bone of Jesus (Ephesians 5); and the Lamb's blood is the life (soul) of Jesus that was "laid down" for His Church.

*John 10:15, NIV: Just as the Father knows me and I know the Father – and I lay down my **life (lit., soul)** for the sheep.*

*Leviticus 17:11, KJV: For the **life (lit., soul)** of the **flesh** is in the **blood***

Jesus laid down His soul for us. The life of the soul is in the blood. The fact that the moon became as blood may also points to the fact that the "whole" Church will exemplify the blood of Jesus that speaks better things, as we learned in the first chapter of this book. The whole moon will one day show off the blood of Jesus to the all the world.

Another application of the "moon becoming as blood" is understood through 2 Kings. The phrase "as blood" is only used one other place in the Scriptures. It is used in 2 Kings 3:22 when water became **"red, as blood."** "Red" in 2 Kings 3:22 is from the Hebrew roots "Adam" which means to show blood in the face.

Thus, effectively, the "moon" became as blood may mean that the whole moon was showing the first Adam's blood on the surface (face) of it. That is, the Church world may one day, negatively, demonstrate the first Adam's nature, in lieu of the last Adam's righteousness. In 2 Kings 3, the context of the water becoming as blood is associated with people potentially killing each other (2 Kings 3:23). This principle also applies to the Church.

Galatians 5:15, NIV: If you keep on biting and devouring each other, watch out or you will be destroyed by each other.

Paul warned the Church not to bite and devour each other. Will there comes a time in history when the whole Church will turn on each other? Will the whole Church be become guilty of destroying one another both spiritually and physically?

The stars that fall like unripe or late figs are the children of the Church who cannot grow because of the dirty leaders. Because there is no light (photosynthesis) for the plants, there will be limited growth. The unripe or late figs were easily shaken and "tossed" by the "mighty wind" of false doctrines (see Ephesians 4:14).

The figs were out of season and exposed as immature figs by the great gale. They should have already been picked for eating; or they may have matured too fast (compare Mark 4:5). However, because of the dirty leaders (no light from the sun), they were not mature properly, thus unripe with "wind of doctrines" at the season of testing.

In the next stage, the heavens were rolled up like a scroll. "Scroll" points to doctrine. The doctrines of heaven will be rolled up. Why? It is time for exposure. The end of mercy ("the great day of His wrath") is at hand, and God is changing the doctrines of the heaven.

"The heavens rolled up" also gives understanding that everything in heaven will be exposed through healthy doctrine. And it does not stop there. The fact that the heavens are ripped open, and God's face and the Lamb's wrath are now exposed means that everything on earth has also been exposed to the face of Him who sits on the throne and the Lamb.

The exposure of all hidden things, including things in heaven, and things in the earth (including people) is the season we are in. This is why "the kings of the earth, the great men, the rich men, the commanders, the mighty men, every slave, and every free man, **hid** themselves in the **caves** and in the **rocks** of the **mountains**...."

God's face is so "dreadful" and "awesome" that every hidden thing is exposed, and every static thing becomes dynamic. The islands (cultic isolated people who do not fellowship with their sister Churches) also have to become dynamic. Have you ever seen an island run? Have you seen a mountain run? Well, this is what happens when the wrath of the Lamb and His face is unveiled.

The exposed men/women had to flee for cover. They fled to the mountains of false churches (church buildings of men) and hid themselves in "rocks" of false-christs (or false believers); and hid themselves in "caves" (or "dens") (Churches that merchandise God's people. In the world there are the mountains of demons, the mountains of religion, and the mountains of flesh.

MOUNTAIN OF DEMONS AND FLESH

*Ezekiel 35:1-3, NKJV: ¹Moreover the word of the LORD came to me, saying, ²"Son of man, set your face against Mount Seir and prophesy against it, ³and say to it, 'Thus says the Lord GOD: "Behold, O **Mount Seir**, I am against you; I will stretch out My hand against you, and make you most desolate.*

"Seir" is defined in the Hebrew as forest, hairy, rough, goat, shaggy, **demon-goat**, to storm (see Strong's Lexicon OT # 8165, 8163 and 8175). Seir is also called a mountain. Seir is the land of Edom or Esau. Paul called Esau's descendants "children of the **flesh**" (Romans 9).

Thus, Mount Seir is a mountain of demons. This same mountain is also a mountain of flesh. It is also a forest mountain full of men who are like beasts (1 Corinthians 15:32). The mountains that are agitated by the Lamb's wrath are the religious mountains of flesh, the mountains of demons, and the roughness of religious systems, mountains of false churches/a pseudo kingdom of God (contrast Isaiah 2:2; Daniel 2:35; 44-45).

Yet, at the same time these are the places where the unbelievers wanted to be hid. They chose "Demon Mountains" rather than God's face, and God's Mountain (Revelation 14; Isaiah 2:1-4). They chose fleshly life rather than the Lamb's mercy. This is true today.

The demonically led assemblies are the ones who hide themselves from the doctrines of the open heaven. They do not fast; they do not want to know about the third day principles. They do not want to mature. They partake of the cup and table of demons, and at the same time, partake of the Lord's Supper (1 Corinthians 10:20-21).

They are hiding in the "caves" ("resorts" or "dens" of thieves that merchandise God's people) and darkness of "rocks" (false-christs). A "rock" is also a symbol of Christ (see 1 Corinthians 10:4). The "caves" are the "dens" described by Jesus in Matthew 21:13. Those who hide from the face of God and the Lamb, there is no light in you. We are called to draw near even when we make mistakes.

WE SHOULD CRY FATHER, FATHER

Romans 8:15, NKJV: For you did not receive the spirit of bondage again to fear, but you received the Spirit of adoption by whom we cry out, "Abba, Father."

When Paul made this statement, he was referring to those who struggle with sin (Romans 7 to Romans 8). Paul's quote above was alluding to the "fear" of Mr. and Mrs. Adam after they sinned. They became "afraid" of the voice of the Lord and "hid" themselves among the trees (Genesis 3:8 w/3:10).

We just discussed the "mountains of forest" where men hid from the face of God and the wrath of the Lamb. Mr. and Mrs. Adam did the same things—"they hid themselves from the presence (lit.; face) of the Lord God among the **trees (forest)...**" (Genesis 3:8). However, for true lambkins this should be opposite.

We should always run **to** God even when we make a mistake. Reading from Romans, Chapter Seven (7) to Chapter Eight (8), we understand that Paul was discussing the shortcoming of sin and how to handle the apparent lack of control. He concluded by saying don't run from God. Instead, cry out to Him as "Father," through the Lamb of God.

"We have not received the spirit of bondage [lit.; slavery] again to fear" (see Romans 8:15). On the contrary, we have "received the Spirit of adoption (lit.; a placed son, Jesus) by Whom we cry, 'Abba, Father'" (see Romans 8:15). This is what Jesus also taught. The evil hates the Light, but "truth" comes to the Light.

*John 3:20-21, NKJV: ²⁰For everyone practicing evil **hates** the light and **does not come** to the light, lest his deeds should be exposed. ²¹But he who does the truth **comes** to the light, that his deeds may be clearly seen, that they have been done in God."*

This is tough. We must learn to always "come" to the light, even though we may feel the temptation to flee because of our mistakes. God is not like some natural fathers. The Lord is opposite. He is approachable. God does not like it when His creation avoids Him (John 1:10-11).

The way for it to be clearly seen that they your deeds have been done in God is to always run to God and the Lamb and cry Father, Father. In other words, even though we are "in God" and make mistakes (I John 1:8); we should come to the light for help (Hebrews 4:16), because we are of the truth.

1 Thessalonians 5:9-11, NKJV: ⁹*For God **did not** appoint us to **wrath**, but to obtain salvation through our Lord Jesus Christ,* ¹⁰*who died for us, that whether we wake or sleep, we should live together with Him.* ¹¹*Therefore **comfort** each other and **edify** one another, just as you also are doing.*

The true Church should not be like the number who "hid" from the face of Him and hid themselves from the Lamb's **passion**. We are "not appointed to wrath." We can "comfort each other and edify one another" in this: "There is therefore now no condemnation to those who are in Christ Jesus..." (Romans 8:1, NKJV).

THE LAMB'S DESIRE

The word "wrath," in Revelation 6:16, is defined as follows according to Strong's Lexicon—Strong's New Testament #3709: properly, **desire** (a reaching forth or excitement of the mind), (by analogy,) violent passion (ire, or justifiable abhorrence); by implication, punishment. This word is translated as anger, vengeance, and indignation.

*John 3:36, NKJV He who believes in the Son has everlasting life; and he who does not believe the Son shall not see life, but the **wrath** of God abides on him."*

What is the strongest desire of the Lamb for humanity? He "desires" that they would receive the everlasting life He procreated for them. Yet, for all He did for humanity, they still ignore Him. Some even call Christians weak. Thus, His "desire" evolves into "desire as reaching forth" — "wrath which abides on" those who do not believe. He is "reaching forth" and uncovering all the secrets of mankind who are not covered by Jesus' blood.

This is why every so often you hear of **exposure** concerning the peoples of the world from rich to poor, from free to slaves. The Lamb's desire is being ignored. Therefore, He exposes their secrets. Yet, as indicated earlier, instead of running to the Lamb, they hide in mountains, caves (or lit.; resorts) and rocks (false-christs), from His face and from the Lamb's desire.

Let the Church be opposite. Let us always approach the Lamb in good circumstances and bad circumstances. His "desire" is to eat the Passover with all who come to Him in humility and repentance.

THE LAMB'S SEVEN HORNS

*Revelation 5:6, NKJV: And I looked, and behold, in the midst of the throne and of the four living creatures, and in the midst of the elders, stood a Lamb...having **seven horns**...which are the **seven Spirits of God** sent out into all the earth.*

*Judges 16:19, NKJV: Then she lulled him to sleep on her knees and called for a man and had him shave off the **seven locks (lit., ringlets of hair) of his head.** Then she began to torment him, and his strength left him.*

Horns denote several things in the Scripture. Horns denote kings; horns denote mountains; horns denote strength, power, and salvation. The Hebrew root word for horns is defined as "to push and "to gore" (Strong's). The Lamb gored the spirit of death through the seven horns (seven Spirits) of resurrection power.

In addition, according to Strong's Concordance, "horn" as used in the New Testament is from a root word that denotes **"hair of the head."** This to me links the **seven horns (or seven hairs of the head)** of the Lamb to the **seven locks (seven ringlets of hair)** of Samson's **head** (Judges 16:19).

Like Samson, the horns (hair) of the Lamb were shaved. However, after three days, the Lamb's horn (hair) grew back and "gored" death in the resurrection of Jesus Christ. The horns (hairs) that were shaved grew back to become the seven horns of salvation.

SHEARED LAMB

*Judges 16:17-19, NKJV [16] And it came to pass, when she pestered him daily with her words and pressed him, so that his **soul was vexed to death**, [17] hat he [Samson] told her all his heart, and said to her, "No **razor** has ever come upon my head, for I have been a Nazarite to God from my mother's* *womb. If I am shaven, then my strength will leave me, and I shall become* ***weak****, and be like any other man."* ¹⁸*When Delilah saw that he had told her all his heart, she sent and called for the lords of the Philistines, saying, "Come up once more, for he has told me all his heart." So, the lords of the Philistines came up to her and brought the money in their hand.* ¹⁹*Then she lulled him to sleep on her knees and called for a man and had him* ***shave off the seven locks of his head****. Then she began to torment him, and* ***his strength left him.***

Acts 8:32, NKJV: ³²*… "He was led as a sheep to the slaughter; and* ***as a lamb before its shearer is silent****, so He opened not His mouth.*

Samson is a type of Christ. In type, Samson lost his seven locks (seven spirits) through seduction of "Delilah." Delilah is a type of "her sin." "Sin" (Gk.; hamartia) in the New Testament is feminine, and the word usually has an article (Gk.; "he," "tees," etc.) in front of it which is also feminine in gender; thus, my phrase "her sin." Jesus came on account of sin to condemn "her sin" (Eve's sin) in the flesh (Romans 8:3).

Delilah seduced Samson, a Nazarene and shaved his seven locks. However, the Lamb willingly laid down Himself to allow His power (hair) to be shaved—"as a lamb before its **shearer** is silent, So He opened not His mouth." Jesus, the Nazarene, willingly allowed His seven hairs (horns) to be shaven for us. In the words of Judges, Jesus' "strength left Him" for a season—"In His humiliation His justice was **taken away**…" (Acts 8:33, NKJV).

Samson's **"soul** was **vexed** to **death,"** which also explains the types of suffering Christ endured on the account of sin. In Matthew 26:38, the Lamb said, "My **soul** is exceedingly **sorrowful**, even to **death**.…" Jesus, the antitype, was under the pressure of mankind's sin to the point of death. (We are and should always be grateful for what He endured for us.)

This is the same thing Delilah did to Samson by her wiles. She vexed him to death. The pressure was so heavy on Jesus that His soul bled. Leviticus states that the life (lit.; "soul") of the flesh is in the blood. Jesus laid down his life (lit.; soul) being obedient to the command of God (John 10:17-18).

Samson in type was also "lulled...to sleep on [sin's] knees." Jesus, the antitype, did not fall asleep on sin's knees. Instead, the Lamb wrestled until His sweat became as blood (Luke 22:39-44). He prayed most of the night, and then willingly allowed His hair (horns) to be shaved by going to the cross for us. The Lamb's words to Peter who wanted to fight for Jesus were: "Permit even this..." (Luke 22:51, NJKV).

What love the Lord has for the Church (His wife). Samson's apparent weakness for Delilah was a type of Christ's love for His Church. He was shaved for us as a Lamb before its shearer. He gave up His Nazarite hair for us. In other words, the Lamb allowed Himself to be shaved by man in order to redeem humanity. This is the greater expression of God's love for us (John 15:13, 1 John 3:16). He became weak in order to strengthen those who would eventually believe in Him. Do you see it?

Samson indicated that he would "become **weak**...like any other man." Peter picks this up in 1 Peter 3:7, in reference to husband and wife. The wife is "weaker;" therefore, the husband must be "weak." In reference to Christ and His Church, the Lamb was "crucified in **weakness**, yet He lives by the power [seven horns] of God..." (2 Corinthians 13:4a).

Samson became weak because he lost his seven locks. Thus, the Lamb became weak for us through crucifixion; yet, like Samson, who grew back his seven locks, the Lamb was raised in power. The Lamb was "sown in **weakness;**" however, He "is raised in power" (see 1 Corinthians 15:43, NKJV). The seven horns (locks) that were shaved were designated to be the horns (hair) of salvation (Luke 1:69).

BORED EYES

Judges 16:21-22, NKJV: ²¹*Then the Philistines took him and **put out** his **eyes and** brought him **down** to **Gaza**. They bound him with **bronze** fetters, and he became a grinder in the prison.* ²²***However, the hair of his head began to grow*** *again after it had been shaven.*

Acts 2:23-24, NKJV: ²³*Him, being delivered by the determined purpose and foreknowledge of God, you have taken by lawless hands, have crucified, and put to death;* ²⁴*whom God raised up, having loosed the pains of death, because it was not possible that He should be **held (lit.; use strength)** by it.*

In type, Samson's eyes got bored out. The Philistines (a type of "ten" wheels on "five axels") put out Samson eyes, and they brought him "down" to a place called "strong" (Gaza) in "bronze" (the serpent's throat[26]). Gaza is a type of the "strength of death" which **was** held by the "serpent" that was eventually rendered inactive by the rebirth (re-growth) of the Lamb's Hair through the power of God.

It may have been dark in death (Job 10:22, no apparent sight for the Lamb); however, the Lamb put His hand to the "grinder" and spun the strength of death to defeat. It was/is impossible for death to hold the Lamb or His lambkins. The Lamb conquered death in a place called "down." He destroyed (rendered inactive) the serpent's throat. Jesus could not see naturally in Death and Hades.

---

[26] See the definition for bronze with its associated roots in Strong's Concordance (OT # 5178, 5154, 5153, 5152).

His natural eyes were shut at His death. However, through the sight of trust in His Father's ability to raise Him from the dead, He destroyed death.

Hebrews 2:14-15, NKJV: *[14]Inasmuch then as the children have partaken of flesh and blood, He Himself likewise shared in the same, that through death He might **destroy** him who had the power (lit.; strength) of death, that is, the devil, [15]and release those who through fear of death were all their lifetime subject to bondage.*

Through His blindness Samson killed more in His death than in His Life. This is another aspect of the Lamb's life that Samson exemplifies. Samson destroyed the house of the Philistines in his death. The Lamb of God conquered the center pillars of the house of Dagon. Through conquering the two middle pillars, more demons were conquered through Jesus' death than before He was crucified.

TWO MIDDLE PILLARS DESTROYED

Judges 16:22-30, NKJV: *[22]**However, the hair of his head began to grow** again after it had been shaven…[30]Then Samson said, "Let me die with the Philistines!" And he pushed with all his might, and the temple fell on the lords and all the people who were in it. So, the dead that **he killed at his death were more than he had killed in his life**.*

The death of Jesus on the cross was a trap for the enemy. Samson's seven locks (seven Spirits) **"began to grow"** again in the prison. When he came to "the middle two pillars" of the Philistines (death and hell), he pushed them over and destroyed the whole idol house of the "fish god" Dagon. The first thing God gave man dominion over was the "fish…" (Genesis 1:28). The Church through Jesus also has dominion over "Dagon," the sea serpent.

This re-growth of Samson's power would be the destruction of Dagon, and the Philistines, a type of rolling demons; and thus, Jesus became the salvation of the world from the bondage of death and hell. Jesus slew (cast out) more demons through His death and resurrection than before He died. Jesus now has the power of the two pillars of the Philistines in His hand.

Judges 16:29-30, NKJV: ²⁹*And Samson took hold of the* **two middle pillars** *which supported the temple, and he braced himself against them, one on his right and the other on his left.* ³⁰*Then Samson said, "Let me die with the Philistines!" And he pushed with all his might, and the temple fell on the lords and all the people who were in it. So, the dead that he killed at his death were more than he had killed in his life.*

Revelation 1:18, NKJV: I am He who lives, and was dead, and behold, I am alive forevermore. Amen. And I have the keys of **Hades and of Death.**

Jesus has the "keys" to Hades and its "gates" (Revelation 1:18 w/Matthew 16:18). He also has the keys of Death and Death's gate (Revelation 1:18 w/Job 38:17). These are the "two middle (or lit.; center) pillars" that Samson pushed over in the resurgence of his seven locks. The Lamb in His resurrection now has the keys of the two middle (center) pillars of the fish god, Satan. The word "center" is linked to resurrection power and/or victory over Death and Hades.

1 Corinthians 15:53-56, NKJV: ⁵³*For this corruptible* **must** *put on incorruption, and this mortal* **must** *put on immortality.* ⁵⁴*So when this corruptible has put on incorruption, and this mortal has put on immortality, then shall be brought to pass the saying that is written:* **"Death is swallowed** *up in victory."* ⁵⁵*"O Death, where is your* **sting**? *O* **Hades, where is your victory?"** ⁵⁶ *The* **sting** *of death is sin, and the strength of sin is the law.*

"Sting" highlighted above is the Greek word "kentron," which is transliterated as "center." Thus, Jesus pushed over the center pillars, Death, and Hades, as Samson pushed over the two "center" pillars of Dagon's house. (Dagon was the **fish** god, which was the half fish, half man.)

Death and Hell is equated to a "great **fish**" (Jonah 1:71 w/Jonah 2:1-2; Matthew 12:40 w/Acts 2:24-27)]. Thus, our Lord did the same things to the pillars of Satan that were mingled with mankind (half demonic, half man). The Lamb rendered them useless and powerless.

Jesus also took the keys for the gates of these entities in victory. "Death (center) is swallowed up in victory," and Hades' victory cannot be found—"O Hades where is your victory?" Hades' victory does not exist anymore. The Lamb (our Greater Samson) pushed over its pillar through His death, burial, and resurrection.

The keys to the gates now belong to Jesus and His Church. We are to use the keys to unlock the nations from the hold of Death (plagues, sword, lack, and beasts) and Hades (fear of the unseen, or that which is demanding). The Church must allow the seven horns of salvation to rise in us in order to convert the three worlds.

HORNS OF SALVATION

*Judges 16:27, NKJV: Now the temple was full of men and women. All the lords of the Philistines were there—**about three thousand men and women** on the roof watching while Samson **performed (lit.; laughed).***

Acts 2:22-41, NKJV: ²²*"Men of Israel, hear these words: Jesus of Nazareth, a Man attested by God to you by miracles, wonders, and signs which God did through Him in your midst, as you yourselves also know —* ²³*Him, being delivered by the determined purpose and foreknowledge of God, you have taken by lawless hands, have crucified, and put to death;*

*²⁴whom God raised up, having loosed the pains of death, because it was not possible that He should be held by it... ³²This Jesus God has raised up, of which we are all witnesses...⁴¹Then those who gladly received his word were baptized; and that day **about three thousand souls** were added to them.*

Samson destroyed the Philistines (who were symbols of demonic spirits). In that day "about three thousand" were on the roof watching Samson "perform" or "laugh." Jesus "laughed" at Death and Hades (compare Psalms 2:4). Even in the middle of Death and Hades, Jesus' was empowered with laughter as His God empowered Him to overcome the two pillars.

The three thousand on the roof (lit.; top) thought they were on "top" of (overcame) Samson. In like manner, the three thousand of the underworld who thought they were on the top became subject to our Greater Samson, the Lamb. After Jesus' resurrection, "about three thousand souls were added to them (the Lord's Church)." In His death Jesus "slew" more from the authority of darkness than before He was crucified.

In other words, the Lamb saved more people after His death and resurrection, than before He was crucified. When Moses gave the Law, three thousand died (Exodus 32:28). When Samson pushed over the two middle pillars, three thousand Philistine men and women, on the roof, died with him. After Jesus was raised from the dead, and after the Holy Spirit was given, three thousand souls were added to the Lord's domain. The Lamb **slew** more in His resurrection than before he was crucified. The Scripture links **"killing a sacrifice"** to salvation.

Acts 10:9-16, NKJV: ⁹... Peter went up on the housetop to pray, about the sixth hour. ¹⁰Then he became very hungry and wanted to eat; but while they made ready, he fell into a trance [1] and saw heaven opened and an object like a great sheet bound at the four corners, descending to him, and *let down to the earth. ¹²In it were all kinds of four-footed animals of the earth, wild beasts, creeping things, and birds of the air. ¹³And a voice came to him, "Rise, Peter; **kill (or sacrifice) and eat."** ¹⁴But Peter said, "Not so, Lord! For I have never eaten anything common or unclean." ¹⁵And a voice spoke to him again the second time, "What God has cleansed you must not call common." ¹⁶This was done three times. And the object was taken up into heaven again.*

Peter indicated that the vision cited above is in reference to the salvation of souls (Acts 11:1-18). Thus, the command for Peter to "kill and eat" is referring to Peter as ministering salvation and fellowshipping with the Gentile Believers. Samson "**killed** at his death more than he had **killed** in his life" (Judges 16:30c, NKJV). The book of Judges gave a specific number of those on the roof — three thousand.

The Lord also **"killed" (saved)** more in His death and resurrection than before His crucifixion. On the day of Pentecost, the Lord saved about three thousand by the mouth of Peter. Saying it another way, through the mouth of Peter, in the Spirit, the Lord slew three thousand demons, so to speak. This was manifested in the natural by about three thousand souls getting saved.

In other words, the Lamb used the keys to open the gates that held humanity bound to the two pillars to the demonic world. The proof is: three thousand were transferred from the domain of Death and Hades to the King's domain of Jesus. The seven horns (seven locks, or seven hairs) that were sheared had re-grown to become that horn of salvation that was spoken of by John, the Baptist's father.

*Luke 1:69-71, NKJV: ⁶⁹And has **raised up** a **horn of salvation** for us in the house of His servant David, ⁷⁰as He spoke by the mouth of His holy prophets, who have been since the world began, ⁷¹that we should be saved from our enemies and from the hand of all who hate us.*

The horn of salvation is Jesus. He is the Lamb of God who has the seven (complete, finished) horns (salvation) for the Church and the world. The salvation of the world is secured in Jesus, the Lamb of God. He has "sent out into all the earth" His "seven horns." The power **for** salvation is in the Holy Spirit of God. The hair of the Lamb is the seven locks—the seven Spirits of God—the Spirit of the Lord, the Spirit of Wisdom, the Spirit of Understanding, the Spirit of Counsel, the Spirit of Power (Force), the Spirit of Knowledge, and the Spirit of the Fear of the Lord (Isaiah 11:1-3).

His Horns have rendered "her sin" inactive by the power of the Holy Spirit. The Lamb of God has destroyed the center pillars and now holds the keys to Death and Hell's gates. The called-out ones is also using these keys to free the bound. Death and sin do not have dominion over the Church or the world anymore; because the prince of this world is judged (Romans 6:9; Romans 6:14 w/John 16:8-11). May the lambkins utilize the power of the Lamb's horns to bring salvation to the world!

Allow your hair to grow with the power of the seven Spirits of God. The manifestation of the hair growth is linked to how the Church "thinks." Note: It was "seven locks of his (Samson's) **head**" (Judges 16:19). "Horn" is defined as "hair of the **head** (Strong's New Testament # 2768).

The head is the place of the mind as learned earlier in the book. Thus, the manifestation of the power of the seven Spirits of God in His lambkins is through the mind of Christ. We must know that our Lord will allow the power of His Spirit to flow in order to bring salvation to the so called three worlds (1st world, 2nd world, and 3rd world nations).

LAMBKINS

*John 21:15, NKJV: So, when they had eaten breakfast, Jesus said to Simon Peter, "Simon, son of Jonah, do you love Me more than these?" He said to Him, "Yes, Lord; You know that I love You." He said to him, "Feed My **lambs**."*

The reference above is the first place the word "lambkin" is used. Jesus called His followers **lambs (lit.; lambkins).** This truth becomes of interest when one sees the only other book that the word lambkin is used. "Lamb," is defined by Strong's Concordance, to mean lambkin, as in the kindred of the Lamb, and is used in the diminutive sense.

It is not the same word translated as "Lamb" in John 1:19. Thus, the Lamb as outlined in the book of Revelation has a twofold meaning. The Lamb is Jesus. The Lamb in the book of Revelation also applies to those who become "like" the Lamb. It relates to those who are the Lamb's kindred. This truth may be strong meat or solid food to some. However, the truth is the truth.

*Hebrews 5:14, NKJV: But solid food belongs to those who are of full age, that is, those who by reason of use have their senses exercised to **discern both good and evil**.*

According to the writer of Hebrews, solid food ("strong meat," KJV) appears to be "evil." This is why one must have his/her **"senses** exercised (trained) to **discern** between good and evil." This ability to tell the difference between good and evil was said in the context of eating the **"meat"** of God's Word. Therefore, meat appears to be evil to some. This is one of the reasons why the Church is still immature. Whenever meat is presented, some think it is evil.

The idea that the "Lamb" in the book of Revelation also applies to the lambkins (those who become like Jesus) may be "evil" to some. This is because to some the idea of becoming like Jesus presents "strong meat" to those who hear it.

However, peoples' opinions do not change the truth of the Scriptures. The Scriptures bear witness to this truth in the Old Testament and the New Testament. To develop this, I will begin with a Scripture that most must acknowledge applies to the Church becoming **like** Jesus.

BECOMING

Ephesians 4:11-14, NKJV: *[11]And He Himself gave some to be apostles, some prophets, some evangelists, and some pastors and teachers, [12]for the equipping of the saints for the work of ministry, for the edifying of the body of Christ, [13]till we all **come to** the unity of the faith and of the knowledge of the Son of God, to a perfect man, to the measure of the stature of the fullness of Christ.*

The phase "come to" means "to arrive at" (we will see a similar definition later used in Daniel relative to One like the Son of Man). We also need to establish "what" and "who" the Saints are striving to come to or to become like.

The "Who" is of course Jesus! The "what" is "maturity" like Jesus! The Saints are maturing to arrive at "the unity of the faith" — moving as a unit with the Lamb and fellow Saints at the same level of faith (trust) that Jesus has.

The Saints are coming to the "knowledge of the Son of God, to a perfect man." The Saints are also perfected through "exact knowledge," not accurate knowledge. There is a difference. The Saints are also becoming "the measure of the stature (age) of the fullness (completion) of Christ." These three goals can be summed up in one sentence. The Saints are reaching, or striving to become **"like"** Her Husband, Jesus. This is logical enough to understand, isn't it?

BE LIKE HIM

*1 John 3:2, NKJV: Beloved, now we are children of God; and it has not yet been revealed what we shall be, but we know that when He is **revealed**, we shall be **like** Him, for we shall **see** Him as He is.*

To the degree He is **"revealed"** to us, is the degree to which we will grow. This is why apostolic and prophetic revelation is of the utmost importance to the Church. We grow to be like Jesus through revelation knowledge that is caught by us or imparted to us by the Lamb. The "revealing," referred to by John, is not just for the future. "He **is** revealed."

"Revealed" is written in the Greek tense voice and mode as aorist, passive, subjunctive. Aorist means that there is no reference to time, duration, or repetition. The aorist tense is usually something that already happened with ongoing results. Jesus already revealed Himself and will reveal Himself again to His Church.

Subjunctive mood refers to something that is contingent upon desire[27], if you desire to be like Him, He will reveal Himself to you. We are like Him **now** to the degree of revelation or the Spirit of revelation that is at work in our lives. Did you notice that when the Lord reveals Himself to us, it becomes special to us; and we tend to purify ourselves even more (1 John 3:3).

---

[27] The subjunctive mood is based upon desire.

AS HE IS

*1 John 4:17, NKJV: Love has been perfected among us in this: that we may have boldness in the Day of Judgment; because **as He is, so are we** in this world.*

As He is, so are we. The same measure that Jesus is, so are we in that measure. John indicated that whatever Jesus is we are the same in this life. We just have to attain to or come to that knowledge experientially. Some put this verse strictly in the future; but that is not the complete truth.

There will be a final Day of Judgment. However, the Day of Judgment also lasts one thousand years. Peter said that one thousand years is as one day (2 Peter 3). Thus, the "Day" of Judgment is also a millennium. In other words, "the millennium rule" is the Day of Judgment which will consummate in a last "day" of that millennium when the final judgment shall be finished.

Saying it another way, in the new millennium to come, the Church who will **not** be taken out of the world, (John 17:15) but will become judges of the world and angels, will be in a new era. The Church will mature to be "as He is…**in this world.**"

Notice, John did not say "outside this world," as in taken somewhere for a time. The Church will judge **"as He"** and through Him **"in this world."** This is in line with the prayer that Jesus prayed in John 17:15. It follows that the Church must mature in love. There comes a time when the baby eagle is forced to fly from the parents nest.

The same is true for the Church. The Lord has carried the Church on His wings because the Church has refused to grow up and fly.

But now, His offspring must grow up and fly. We are His offspring; we are His kindred, and we must become "like Him.

GOD'S LIKENESS

*Genesis 1:26, NKJV: Then God said, "Let Us make man in Our image, according to Our **likeness**; let them have dominion....*

It should not be strange that we are to become "like" Jesus. Jesus — the last Adam — is the only one who walked in the original "likeness" of God; and we are to become that "likeness" again that the first Adam lost. When Mr. and Mrs. Adam were tempted, they were tempted to be something/someone that they already were.

*Genesis 3:4-5, NKJV: [4]Then the serpent said to the woman, "You will not surely die. [5]For God knows that in the day you eat of it your eyes will be opened, and you will be **like** God, knowing good and evil.*

Wait a minute. Did I read right? Was the enemy trying to get Adam to be "like God?" The influence of the serpent must have been strong for Mr. and Mrs. Adam to forget that they were already "like God" — "God said, Let Us make man in...Our **likeness**...." Therefore, they were **already** like God. They must have forgotten the fact of their place of dominion over the serpent.

Somehow the serpent was able to make them desire to be something they already were. Doesn't this sound familiar? There are a lot of people who do not know about or believe in the "finished work" of Jesus. We are already restored as gods of the earth.

Yet, they are being deceived to keep the old image of the fallen Adam, which is a fallen state, a state (likeness) of fear, defeat, and failure. You can tell when the "finished work" of Jesus' likeness is not operational in people's lives, when they rarely "finish" (complete) any endeavors. Some do not "finish" their walk with God. They go back to hiding from God in the womb of fear. The likeness of the first Adam is still more real to them than the likeness of the last Adam—Jesus.

Genesis 5:1-3, NKJV: [1]*... God created man, He made him in the **likeness of God**. *[2]*He created them male and female and blessed them and called **them** Mankind (lit.; Adam) in the day **they** were created.* [3]*And Adam ... **begot a son in his own likeness**, after his image, and named him Seth.*

Adam was indeed created in the "likeness of God." However, after his fall from dominion, he began to birth children "in his **own** likeness...." "His own likeness" is a likeness of being dominated by deception rather than "Mankind" defining their dominion in the earth.

By Scriptural definition "all things are yours [the Church's]...the world or life or death or things present or things to come—all are yours [the Church's]" (1 Corinthians 3:21-22). You can command dead things to give life to you. You can command the "world" to release your provision. If you see danger in "things to come," you can redirect the danger. The same is true for any other "things present" we may need.

Psalm 82:6, NKJV: [6]*I said, "You are **gods**, and all of you are children of the Most High.* [7]*But you shall die like men and fall like one of the princes."*

John 10:34-36, NKJV: [34]*Jesus answered them, "Is it not written in your law, 'I said, "**You are gods**" '?* [35]*If He called them gods, to whom the word of God came (**and the Scripture cannot be broken**),* [36] *do you say of Him whom the Father sanctified and sent into the world, 'You are blaspheming,' because I said, 'I am the Son of God'?*

Adam was a god. He was in the likeness of the God. The same is true today for those "to whom the word of God came; and according to Jesus; "The Scripture cannot be broken." The Word of God comes to the Church; and no one can break the truth that Believers in the Church are gods of the earth.

Note: being gods of the earth does **not** make us gods of other people. No one is to lord over another human. Before Adam fell from his dominion as god of the earth, he defined and dominated entities like the serpents. He was a god to the serpent.

The earth's resources also belonged to Mr. and Mrs. Adam and all their children. However, after their fall from that place of rulership, Adam (both of "them") was being redefined by the new likeness he/she took on—the likeness of self-consciousness, in lieu of the likeness of God-consciousness. This is one of the greatest fight of humanity—the fight of not being so self-conscious of weakness. This cripples one from attaining any degree of spiritual or natural accomplishment in life.

*Genesis 3:7, NKJV: Then the eyes of both of them were opened, and **they knew that they were naked;** and they sewed fig leaves together and made themselves coverings.*

Without going into detail, the first thing that Mr. and Mrs. Adam realized after eating from the tree was that they were naked. They became self-conscious. They were not conscious of their being in the likeness of God they were previously designed to be. The fatal result was that the false sensation of self-consciousness was then imparted to their children.

This is the trouble for most today, most have an image problem. Most are being dominated by someone else's idea of likeness (the serpents,' other people) rather than the likeness of God. The **recreated** man in the likeness (image) of God is one of the things that Jesus restored to humanity.

*Colossians 3:10, NKJV: And have put on the new man who is renewed in knowledge according to the **image** of Him who **created** him.*

We are a "new" creation in God. Jesus is "the Beginning of the (new) creation of God" (Revelation 3:14, NKJV). We are recreated in Jesus' likeness and image. We are like the Son of Man through the creation act; and that likeness is to become an experiential truth in us and through us, which means, we will be as gods on the earth again and dominate in life, because of one Man, Jesus Christ.

ONE LIKE THE SON OF MAN

*Daniel 7:13, NKJV: I was watching in the night visions, and behold, **One like the Son of Man**, coming with the clouds of heaven! He came to the **Ancient of Days**, and they brought Him near before Him.*

Notice that the Scripture states "One **like** the Son of Man. Who is the "Son of Man? Jesus is the Son of Man (see Matthew, Mark, Luke, John, and Acts). The logical question then is, "Who is this person that is **"like** the Son of Man?"

It has to be whoever has matured into that "perfect **man**, to the measure of the **stature** of the fullness (completion) of Christ (Ephesians 4:13). It has to be whoever that "one new man" (Ephesians 2:15). What are the characteristics of this **"perfect man," this "one new man?"**

This **"man"** that Paul alluded to is made up of all Believers. The Ones **like** the Son of Man are those who rule on earth in the righteous manner in which God originally created us to rule. It is the corporate "new man" that has been restored into the image of God (Colossians 3:10 and Ephesians 4:24). "We … are being transformed into the same image" as Jesus (see 2 Corinthians 3:18; Hebrews 2:5-9). We are becoming **like** His **"stature" (lit.; age).**

Daniel also made an interesting statement in reference to the "One like the Son of Man." The "One like the Son of man" was presented before the "Ancient of Days." This "Ancient of Days" is Jesus. The "Ones like the Son of Man" are the mature ones in the Church who are presented to Jesus for rulership of the nations.

"Ancient of Days" literally reads "Weaned of Days." The Hebrew word "attiyq" (at-teek') is also used for babies that are drawn (weaned) from the breast and is defined as "weaned" by Strong's Concordance.

*Isaiah 28:9, NKJV: "Whom will he teach knowledge? And whom will he make to understand the message? Those just weaned from milk? Those just **drawn** from the **breasts**?*

For babies to be weaned from the breast, they had to have partaken of breast milk. For the "Ancient of Days" to be "weaned from days," He had to have lived in time. This is Jesus. He came from eternity and lived in the daytime.

He then had to be weaned from the time realm and restored to His original glory, the glory of the "Ancient of Days." Thus, Jesus is the One on the Throne who gave the kingdoms of the earth to His mature Believers—those who have "come forth to" be **"like"** Him, and as Him in the earth.

ONE LIKE THE SON OF MAN IN THE SEVEN LAMPSTANDS

Revelation 1:12-13, NKJV: ¹²Then I turned to see the voice that spoke with me. And having turned I saw seven golden lampstands, ¹³ and in the midst of the seven lampstands One like the Son of Man, clothed with a garment down to the feet and girded about the chest with a golden band.

John "heard" a voice as a trumpet. This voice could also be "seen;" because John "turned to **see** the voice that spoke." This voice is the

Son of Man, Head (Christ Jesus) and Body (Christ, the Church — 1 Corinthians 12:12).

This is understood from the statement made by John. He called the "voice" "One **like** the Son of Man." "Like" is the Greek word "homoios" which is from the root "homo" or "hama." "Homoios," with its roots "homo" and "hama," means: "the same, (along with, at the same time, similar, close association).

Thus, the "One **like** the Son of Man" is Jesus in the midst of His Church; and He is also the corporate man who is a "close associate" of Jesus. The Head (Jesus) and His Body (the Church) "at the same time" is that "Son of Man." This may be strong meat for some; however, it is the truth.

Let me say this another way; Jesus divided Himself (His full measure) into five parts. The apostles, prophets, evangelists, pastors, and teachers are the five measures that total up the measure of Christ. Jesus then commissioned these five measures (offices, ministries) to bring the Church to the same measure as Christ gave them. Thus, the five ministry gifts are the ones who are like the Son of Man; and eventually the Church as a whole will also become like Christ experientially.

*Ephesians 4:7-13, NKJV: ⁷But to each one of us grace was **given** according to the **measure** of Christ's gift…¹¹And He Himself **gave** some to be apostles, some prophets, some evangelists, and some pastors and teachers, ¹²for the equipping of the saints for the work of ministry, for the edifying of the body of Christ, ¹³till we all **come** to the unity of the faith and of the knowledge of the Son of God, to a perfect man, to the **measure** of the stature of the fullness of Christ.*

Paul said that "grace was **given** according to the **measure** of Christ." **Jesus** "gave" the measure of Himself to His apostles, prophets, evangelists, pastors, and teachers. These five separate measures make up the total measure of Jesus. Thus, the five gifts are "like" Jesus. They can only bring the Church to that measure of Jesus because they (combined) have the measure. This measure is mature love Jesus defined in John 13:24, John defined in 1 John 3:16 and Paul defined in 1 Corinthians 13.

That is, they cannot mature the Church to be **like** Christ's love unless they themselves are indeed **like** Christ in demonstrating His love. A man of God can only bring you to the "measure" he has attained to or has been gifted with. Thus, it takes a corporate man with a corporate measure to mature the Church.

There is "One like the Son of Man" in the middle of the lampstand who will bring the Church to the "measure" of that "perfect Man," Jesus. That "one" includes the Head (Jesus) and the Body of Christ (the Church). Now I would like to close this chapter with this.

The intent of this chapter was just to introduce the concept of the Church being **like** Christ, especially related to His love for us. I will not develop the subject in detail. Some may think I am mad to say that the "One like the Son of Man" is made up of Jesus and those who are like Jesus. Nonetheless, I pray that the reader will be like those of Berea. They were "fair-minded…in that the received the word…and searched the Scriptures daily to find out whether these things were so" (Acts 17:11).

THE LAMB'S LIGHT

*Revelation 21:23, NKJV: The city had no **need (lit., employment)** of the sun or of the moon to shine in it, for the glory of God illuminated it. The **Lamb** is its **light**.*

Three types of lights are noted above. There is the "shine" of the sun and moon. The "illumination" of God's glory is also a light. Thirdly, the Lamb is the City's portable light.

SUN AND MOON

*Revelation 21:23, NKJV: The city had no **need (lit.; employment)** of the sun or of the moon to sine in it....*

First, we must understand that "the city" is New Jerusalem, which was developed in a previous chapter in this book. In this city, a time came when the "shine" of the sun and moon was not necessary. This can be looked at from a natural perspective, meaning that the natural light of the sun and moon will one day be "unemployed" for light.

However, the sun and the moon means something more. First of all, natural lambs are not light bearers. Thus, as the Lamb is symbolic of "light," so the sun and moon are symbolic. Yes, God's glory and the Lamb's light is so real and powerful that their glory can lighten the whole earth (Ezekiel 43:1-2, Revelation 18:1, etc.). Yet, the sun and the moon can also be functions of people.

*Genesis 37:9-11, NKJV: [9]Then he dreamed still another dream and told it to his brothers, and said, "Look, I have dreamed another dream. And this time, the **sun**, the **moon**, and the **eleven stars** bowed down to me." [10]So he told it to his father and his brothers; and his father rebuked him and said to him, "What is this dream that you have dreamed? Shall your* *mother and **I** and **your brothers** indeed come to bow down to the earth before you?"*

Here we see that the sun, moon, and stars are people. Jacob is the sun. His wife (woman) is the moon. Jacob's twelve children are the stars. The light of the sun is the light of **fathers (elders (Gk.; presbuteros))** in the Church, or masculine leaders in general.

The light of the moon is the light of the **mothers (older women (Gk.; "presbutis," feminine of "presbuteros"))** in the Church, or feminine leaders in general. Therefore, according to Revelation 21:23, there will come a time when the sun and moon will no longer be needed.

*Titus 2:3, NKJV: The **older women (presbutis)** likewise, that they be reverent in behavior, not slanderers, not given to much wine, **teachers** of good things.*

*1 Peter 5:1, NKJV: The **elders (presbuteros)** who are among you I exhort, **I who am a fellow elder (sumpresbuteros)** and a witness of the sufferings of Christ, and also a partaker of the glory that will be revealed.*

There will come a time when the "shine" of the elder women and elder men will not be needed. These elder women (presbutis and elder men (presbuteros) include the fivefold ministries. Yes, I believe in having women elders. Paul also worked with "**presbutis**;" and they are "teachers" along with the masculine presbyters. Currently, we do need our "**presbutis**" (elder women) and our "presbyters" (elder men).

We do need the supply of the measures of the men and women leaders in the Church. Again, I am not saying that the Church is to the place where the fathers and mothers will not be needed. What I am saying is their light will eventually not be employed for lighting the city; the Lamb's light is and will be the light the city.

The five ministries of Ephesians 4:11 were given **"till."** "Till" or until is a "time" word. They were given until the Church matures, according to Ephesians 4:11-13. Thus, when the time comes that the city does not need the sun and the moon anymore; this means that the Church has matured to the point where the Lamb has now become her light. She has the ability to release the Lamb's light through her body, for herself and for the nations.

THE RAYS OF GOD'S GLORY

Revelation 21:23, NKJV: The city had no need of the sun or of the moon to shine in it, for the glory of God illuminated it....

We have discussed earlier that the Church (New Jerusalem) having the glory of God means that she has a sin-free life. We now learn that this same glory "illuminates," that is, the glory of God sheds rays of light, according to the Greek definition.

The sun and the moon were no longer needed because the illumination of God's glory has finally been seen. His rays are finally shining through, because of a sin-free life. Sin is an obstruction of light. Sin causes a person to occlude God's glory. Sin conceals God's glory (good opinion), and sin is inferior to God's glory.

*Romans 3:23, NKJV: For all have sinned and **fall short** of the glory of God.*

*Genesis 3:7, NKJV: Then the eyes of both of them were opened, and they knew that they were naked; and they sewed fig leaves together and made themselves **coverings**.*

*Genesis 3:10, NKJV: So, he said, "I heard Your voice in the garden, and I was afraid because I was naked; and I **hid** myself."*

The Greek word for "fall short" used in Romans 3 cited above also means "inferior." Therefore, sin is inferior to God's glory. Relative to "light," sin is inferior. Saying it another way, sin is inferior lighting to the illumination of God's glory. Therefore, when the city had the glory of God (Revelation 21:11), it also means that she had superior lighting in her city. Her lighting could be seen. She was not hidden.

Jesus said it this way: "You are the light of the world. A **city** that is set on a **hill** cannot be **hidden**" (Matthew 5:14). Jesus called His disciples (Church) a city. The hill that this city is set on is Mount Zion; and the world must see her "light." Her lighting is God's glory. The light is not "hidden" because she is sin-free.

Mr. and Mrs. Adam "hid" themselves from the presence of God. They also covered themselves. This is what sin does; it causes one to cover God's glorious illumination. New Jerusalem did not need the light of the sun and moon anymore.

God's illumination was able to be seen in them. There will come a time when the leader of the Church will not be needed as **"ruling"** lights (compare Genesis 1:16). The ruling light will be God's illumination. The whole city will be full of light, the light of the glory of God.

THE WHOLE BODY FULL OF LIGHT

Matthew 6:22-23, NKJV: *²²The lamp of the body is the eye.* ***If therefore your eye is good (lit., folded together), your whole body will be full of light.*** *²³But if your eye is bad, your whole body will be full of darkness. If therefore the light that is in you is darkness, how great is that darkness!*

I will try to keep this as brief as possible. "Good" (NKJV) or "single" (KJV) means to be folded together. Mr. and Mrs. Adam's natural eyes were open. However, their spiritual eyes were "folded" to evil before they were opened to bad by the enticement of the enemy. It was after the serpent's enticement, she "**saw** that the tree was good for food, that it was pleasant to the eyes..." (Genesis 3:6). Also, after they ate, "the **eyes** of both of them were **opened**..." (Genesis 3:7a).

God made the tree and put it off limits. In addition, the Lord in His wisdom blinded (folded together) their spiritual eyes to the tree. So, the desire to eat from the tree would not be aroused. Their eyes were then reopened to good **and** evil by the wrong entity and before "time." Jesus came to tell us that our eyes should be "folded together" again.

The purpose is that a "folded eye" will cause us to be full of light. This light is the glory of God and the Lamb's light. Jesus wants the "whole body" of Christ to be "full of light." This is a sin-free life where the glory of God illuminates the whole city (Church).

I get excited just thinking about this. One day the "whole" Church will only be illuminated with God's glory and the Lamb's light. The Church will become independent of roaming lights (sun and moon) and be dependent on the eternal light of God's glory and the "true light" of the Lamb.

Now even though we will eventually not need the sun and the moon, the sun and the moon are related to God's glory that is released through the city. The illumination of God's glory is related to three (3) things (the quality of Jesus, the quality of Spirit and the quality of gospel) imparted by the sun (male leaders) and the moon (female leaders) to the Church via the mind. The eyes that have to be folded together are the eyes of our mind.

*2 Corinthians 11:3, NKJV: But I fear, lest somehow, as the serpent deceived Eve by his craftiness, so your **minds** may be corrupted from the **simplicity** (lit.; **folded together**) that is in Christ.*

As I stated earlier, the serpent is the culprit that causes the eyes not to be folded together. This is done through the "mind." Thus, mindsets are related to God's glory. In fact, "glory" is defined as good **opinion** or good **thought**, according to Greek lexicons.

Therefore, the mind is the avenue by which a "single" or "good" eye can be realized, which will result in God's glory filling the whole body. With this established, and as indicated earlier, the things that are related to God's glory illuminating us and shining through us is the type of Jesus that is being preached to you, the type of spirit you receive, and the quality of gospel that is preached to you.

*2 Corinthians 11:4, NKJV: For if he who comes preaches **another**[28] Jesus whom we have not preached, or if you receive a **different** spirit which you have not received, or a **different** gospel which you have not accepted....*

2 Corinthians 11:4 is a continuation of Paul's subject on "simplicity." Therefore, the current ways that the serpent affects the eyes of the Church are by the leaders (sun and the moon) who preach "another Jesus," and leaders who cause the Church to "receive a different spirit" other than the Holy Spirit; leaders who declare a "different gospel."

Thus, the singleness, simplicity or good that causes the Body of Christ to be full of light (the light of God's glory and the light of the Lamb) is linked to the quality of Jesus, the quality of Spirit and the quality of gospel being imparted by the Elders and presbutis (women elders) of God.

Therefore, they (the sun and moon) are important. The sun and the moon are means to an end. They are not the end. The end is the

---

[28] Note: preaching "'another-same' Jesus" relates to preaching Jesus relative to nationalism, race, pedigree, and so on.

Lamb's Light and God's glorious illumination becoming the manifest Light. The day when the Church becomes sin-free, they (presbuteros and presbutis) will not be employed to give light. As stated before, the Glory of God on the inside of us is the illumination in the city of God. The whole city is full of light.

THE LAMB IS THE LIGHT

*Revelation 21:23, NKJV: The city had no **need (lit.; employment)** of the sun or of the moon to shine in it, for the glory of God illuminated it. The **Lamb** is its **light**.*

"Light" is translated as "portable lamp." The city utilized the Lamb's light as its portable light. This light will be so bright that according to Isaiah, the moon will be "disgraced" and the sun "ashamed." This means that eventually all the so called super apostles will be marginalized by the greater light of the Lamb.

All the self-made prophets will be superseded by the greater light of the Lamb. All the evangelists who refuse to submit to true authority, in the sense of Acts 8, will be superseded by the Lamb's light. The light of the pastors and teacher will have to give way to the light of the Lamb.

The five gifts of Ephesians 4:11 were given "till" the Church matures to be like Jesus. Once this is accomplished, the Lamb Himself will be the light of the Church. This means that the many parts will become obsolete in the perfected whole. That which is in part must give way to that which is perfect.

1 Corinthians 13:10-11, NKJV: [10]But when **that** which is **perfect** has come, then that which is in **part** will be done away. [11]When I was a child, I spoke as a child, I understood as a child, I thought as a child; but when I became a **man**, I put away childish things.

"That which is perfect" is Jesus, is Love. When the Perfect One is perfected in us, all the leaders as we know them will not be employed anymore. When the "child" becomes like the "Man," "childish things" will be "put away." The sun and the moon will eventually be replaced with the mature light of the Lamb. This light is the Life of God.

THE LIFE IS LIGHT

*John 1:4, NKJV: In Him was life, and the **life** was the **light** of men.*

The Lamb being the "Light" also has to do with Jesus being the "Life" of the Church. Remember, New Jerusalem is a **living** city. The city lives by the Lamb. The "stones" of the city are "living stones" (2 Peter 2:5). The city with foundations that Abraham looked for is New Jerusalem. These foundations are people (Revelation 21:14, Hebrews 11:10; and Ephesians 2:20).

One of the applications of the "gates" of New Jerusalem is that the gates are hearts or souls (living things) of people (see the Hebrew definition for Proverbs 23:7). And for more proof that everything that God makes is living, the horns of the altar "spoke" in Revelation 9:13.

My point is, everything in New Jerusalem is living and needs life. The Lamb Himself supplies this "Life." Jesus' life-style is the Light to the city and the light to the rest of humanity. There will be no need for the sun and the moon. The **life**-style of Jesus is Light. Remember Peter's reaction to the Lord when Peter saw the great catch of fishes. He felt **astonished (lit.; stupefy, dumbfounded)** asking Jesus (the Life) to "depart" from him because he Peter, was "sinful" (Luke 5:1-9). Peter felt ashamed. Why? Because he was a professional fisherman; and he could not catch "one" fish after fishing all night.

The moon shall be "disgraced," and sun shall be "ashamed" when the Lord's Light is manifested in full radiance in Jerusalem (Isaiah 24:23). The Lord's Light (Life) will rule gloriously before His elders (the sun and moon). The ability of the Lamb's light to shine in His city is important. His light affects nations. That means that the ability of the Church to employ the Light of the Lamb has national implications.

Revelation 21:24-26, NKJV: [24]*And the **nations of those who are saved**[29] shall walk in its **light**, and the kings of the earth bring their glory and honor into it.* [25]*Its gates shall not be shut at all by day (there shall be **no night** there).* [26]*And they shall bring the glory and the honor of the **nations** into it.*

The Light of the Lamb has **national implications**. The nations walk in the Lamb's light. This is why when the Church hides in four walls it does not have the right attitude. The Church should also allow the nations to be enlightened by the Lamb's Light or Life. The glory of the kings (political leaders) of the earth and their nations will bring their glory and "value" to the Church when they see the Light of the Lamb. The Lamb's light will cause "no night [to be] there."

Night in Scripture points to drunkenness (spiritual and natural) and sleeping (not watching in prayer) (see 1 Thessalonians 5:7 and Mark 14:37-38). The night will not be there because the Light (Life, the same Life Jesus lived) will be evident in the city of the living God.

This Life (Light) will be attractive to political leaders, and the nations they lead will bring glory (lit., good opinion) and honor

---

[29] Note the Majority Texts and the Alexandrian Text omit the phrase "of those who are saved" in Revelation 21:24.

(lit., value, money) into the City of the Lamb. I look forward to the day, and the day has already begun, when political leaders and the nations will speak well of the true Church. I look forward to when they will bring their value to the Lamb in His city. Remember the Lamb is **the** Light of the City of God; and His goal is to teach and disciple the nations. Amen!

THE LAMB IS THE TEMPLE

Revelation 21:22, NKJV: But I saw no temple in it, for the Lord God Almighty and the Lamb are its temple.

The book of Revelation seems "closed" to some. However, if a person can see beyond the apparent enigmas the book can be understood. In fact, as established earlier in this book, the book of Revelation is an open book. Some are teaching the book of Revelation from a natural (soulish) standpoint, meaning, they are not "comparing spiritual things with spiritual" through the Holy Spirit (1 Corinthians 2:13). Thus, the truth looks like "foolishness" (absurd) to them; and they teach absurdity (1 Corinthians 2:14).

Thus, when one reads the verse above it should not seem strange that the Lamb is one aspect of the temple, and the Lord God Almighty is another aspect of the temple. There is no man-made temple building in New Jerusalem. This temple is not made with hands. "...Christ came as High Priest of the good things to come, with the greater and more perfect **tabernacle not made with hands,** that is, not of this creation (Hebrews 9:11, NKJV).

With that said, my express purpose in this chapter is not to discuss the temple from the standpoint of "the Lord God Almighty," or the lambkins. I only say that the temple, as it relates to the "Lord God Almighty," has to do with the availability of God's "All-power;" and God's "All-strength," through Jesus' being both "Lord" (Supreme) and "God" (Self existing/sustaining One, Creator) to His Church for the purpose of ruling the nations. The Lord God Almighty is also the equal essence of the temple along with the Lamb.

So, what does it mean that the Lamb is the temple of the City — New Jerusalem? The natural temple is a place of worship, is it not? Thus, the Lord God and the Lamb constitute that place of worship.

THE PLACE OF WORSHIP

*John 4:21, NKJV: Jesus said to her, "Woman, believe Me, the hour is coming when you will **neither** on this **mountain**, **nor** in **Jerusalem**, worship the Father.*

There was an issue in the days of Jesus with regard to the place of worship. The natural Jews said that Jerusalem was the place. The Samaritan believed that "Sychar" was the place. The same beliefs are true today.

There are many reputed man-made places of worship. Yet, Jesus refuted all of these arguments. He said, "you will **neither** on this **mountain, nor** in **Jerusalem**, worship the Father." Jesus then gave them the "place" of worship.

*John 4:23, NKJV: But the hour is coming, and **now is,** when the true worshipers will worship the Father **in spirit** and **truth**; for the Father is seeking such to worship Him.*

The place of worship is in "spirit and truth." Both the Spirit and Truth are personified. Truth is both Jesus and the Holy Spirit. The Spirit is also the Spirit of Jesus. The place of worshipping God is in the Son and in the Holy Spirit. As Revelation says, "The Lord **God Almighty [God is Spirit]** and **the Lamb [the Son]** are its temple."

*Philippians 3:3, NKJV: For we are the circumcision, **who worship God in the Spirit,** rejoice in Christ Jesus, and have no confidence in the flesh*

*John 14:6, NKJV: Jesus said to him, "I am… **the truth**.…"*

*John 15:26, NKJV: But when the Helper comes…the **Spirit of truth** who proceeds from the Father, He will testify of Me.*

*Philippians 1:19, NKJV: For I know that this will turn out for my deliverance through your prayer and the supply of **the Spirit of Jesus Christ**.*

Therefore, as our Lord indicated, the place of worship is "Spirit" — a person — and "Truth" — also a person. Paul also stated the same thing in Philippians 3:3 above. The place of worshipping God is in the Spirit which is also the Truth. The hour of worshipping God in Spirit **"now is."**

There are many that go to a building to worship. However, if the congregation is not in Spirit and in Truth, they are in the wrong place of worship. You see, the place of worship is not a physical location.

Worship is a state of being in the Spirit of Jesus. Yet, we do not forsake the assembling of ourselves, according to the book of Hebrews 10:25. On the contrary, we should meet regularly — 1 Corinthians 11:26.)

Worshipping God in Spirit is not people "jerking" in Church and bucking like bulls. God did not give the Spirit to worship Him with "bucking" like animals. Worshipping in Spirit means we should worship from the heart.

Worshipping in the Truth means we should worship with our hands and body, and I do not mean jerking and bucking like animals. Religious antics have made the Church distasteful. There is a correct way to worship with the hands and heart.

HEART AND HANDS

*Lamentations 3:41, NKJV: Let us lift our **hearts** and **hands** To God in heaven.*

Worshiping God from the heart is worshipping God in Spirit. No one can see your heart unless the Lord reveals. Therefore, you have to be true to yourself. Lifting up your open hands is worshipping God in the truth. Yes, truth says to use the members of your body to worship God. We can use instruments to worship God. But truth also says it must be from the heart, in the Spirit.

There are many who worship with their hands, yet their hearts are far from God. Thus, Jesus in His infinite wisdom stated that true worship is both in Spirit and in Truth. If one of the two is missing (Spirit or Truth) then a congregation or an apparent worshipper is not in that place (state) of true worshipping.

The apparent bucking and jerking can be tempered with the Truth. When David danced before the Ark, he danced with "his might." He was not "overtaken" by some spirit and bucking like an animal. For those who have no movements at all, the dead, dry worship of no spiritual touch can be made alive by Spirit.

Spirit and Truth in worship are twins and one cannot do without the other in worship. The state of worship is both using the body like dancing, lifting of the hand, etc. and using the Spirit like spontaneous songs of the Lord, integrating heart with body movements, etc. In Spirit and in Truth also means spontaneity, as the Lord wills.

1 Timothy 2:8, NKJV: I desire therefore that the men pray everywhere, lifting up holy hands, without wrath and doubting.

We can "pray **everywhere**" by "lifting up holy hands" (for those who are able to). This signifies that the place of worship is not a physical place. The place is where the Lord's wills. The verse above implies that an urging to worship "everywhere" must have come from the Holy Spirit; hence, Paul's encouragement not to "doubt" and not to be "angry." Why?

It is a little easier for some to worship in a building. However, for some it is very embarrassing to lift the hands and pray "everywhere," which must sometimes include a public setting. I also understand that there are some on the other end of the spectrum.

They (modern Pharisees) love to pray and worship in public to be seen by men. Jesus, said not to follow men who do religious things in public to be seen. What Paul is refereeing to is true worship in Spirit as the Lord leads. Sometimes worship that is heard by the unsaved brings salvation to them. We must be willing to confess our Lord's name and praise everywhere.

*Acts 16:25-34, NKJV: 25But at midnight Paul and Silas were **praying** and **singing hymns** to God, and the **prisoners** were **listening** to them. 26Suddenly there was a great earthquake, so that the foundations of the prison were shaken; and immediately all the doors were opened, and everyone's chains were loosed. 27And the keeper of the prison, awaking from sleep and seeing the prison doors open, supposing the prisoners had fled, drew his sword and was about to kill himself. 28But Paul called with a loud voice, saying, "Do yourself no harm, for we are all here." 29Then he called for a light, ran in, and fell down trembling before Paul and Silas. 30And he brought them out and said, "Sirs, what must I do to be saved?" 31So they said, "Believe on the Lord Jesus Christ, and you will be saved, you and your household." 32Then they spoke the word of the Lord to him and to all who were in his house. 33And he took them the same hour of the night and washed their stripes. And immediately he and all his family were baptized. 34 Now when he had brought them into his house, he set* *food before them; **and he rejoiced, having believed in God with all his household.***

Prison is certainly not Church. Yet Paul and Silas prayed and worshiped after being whipped for casting out a demon. The Lamb was their temple; and this "temple" of the Lamb is mobile. He is with us everywhere we may end up. Paul and Silas went to the place of worship, the place in the Lamb, the place in Spirit and in Truth. The result was salvation.

If what happened to Paul and Silas happened to most in the Church today, instead of going to the temple of the Lamb in Spirit and in Truth, they probably would think that God hates them, or they did something wrong. No, beloved, we must be willing to lift our hands and our hearts to God "everywhere." Why? "The Lord is there," in us.

*Ezekiel 48:35, NKJV: All the way around shall be eighteen thousand cubits; and the name of the **city** from that day shall be: **The LORD Is There**.*

Ezekiel saw a city. I am aware how scholars have tried to explain the city and the temple as a building. However, what Ezekiel saw was a Person as the temple and a people as the city. The name of this city is "The Lord is there."   Yes, the Lord is there because the **Lord** God Almighty and the **Lamb** are the temple, or place of worship. The called-out ones must mature to worship in the temple of the Lamb "everywhere."   In Spirit and in Truth we should worship on our "beds" (Psalms 149:5) the night before we gather corporately. We should be singing with grace in our hearts to the Lord (Colossians 3:16) while we are going about. Why? "The Lord is (always) there" in us.

Did you know that Job teaches that God sometime moves all around us and does not make Himself known to us? Thus, even when we think that He is not there, we should worship in Spirit and in Truth because He **"is there."** He is the place or state of worship. In the City of God, the Lord God Almighty and the Lamb are the temple—the place and state or worship.

John said that he "saw **no** temple in it, for the Lord God Almighty and the Lamb are its temple (Revelation 21:22, NKJV). Again, for emphasis, which is "not tedious" for me, "but for you it is safe" (Philippians 3:1), John "saw no (natural) temple" in New Jerusalem—the Church. The temple that he saw was different from the emphasis of today's man-made temples. The temple was the Lamb of God and the Lord God Almighty. The Lamb is the "temple." Amen.

THE TEMPLE OF JESUS' BODY

*John 2:19-21, NKJV: [19]Jesus answered and said to them, "Destroy this **temple**, and in three days I will raise it up." [20]Then the Jews said, "It has taken forty-six years to build this temple, and will You raise it up in three days?" [21]But He was speaking of the **temple of His body.***

Jesus Himself declared that His body is the temple. He purged the natural temple building which has its place. However, He also established the true temple, the temple of His body. The same John, who wrote the verse above, penned the book of Revelation. The Lamb is the temple which Jesus declared before His death, burial, and resurrection. He is our Sacrifice and our place of sacrifice. He is the Living Temple. He is the living altar. Amen!

*Hebrews 13:10-13, NKJV: [10]We have an **altar** from which those who serve the tabernacle have no right to eat. [11]For the bodies of those animals, whose blood is brought into the sanctuary by the high priest for sin, are burned outside the camp. [12]Therefore Jesus also, that He might sanctify the people with His own blood, suffered outside the gate. [13]Therefore let us go forth to **Him**, outside the camp, bearing His reproach.*

THE LAMB'S BOOK OF LIFE

*Philippians 4:3, NKJV: And I urge you also, true companion, help these women who **labored (lit.; wrestled)** with me in the gospel, with Clement also, and the rest of my **fellow workers**, whose names are in **the Book of Life**.*

*Revelation 3:5, NKJV: He who **overcomes** shall be clothed in white garments, and I will **not** blot out his name from **the Book of Life;** but I will confess his name before My Father and before His angels.*

The Book of Life carries a serious overtone in some of its references. The name of the Book of Life appears in conjunction with not worshiping the beast, the lake of fire, the inability to enter New Jerusalem, and so on. It is first mentioned in the New Testament with words like "wrestle" and "overcome" as seen above. This chapter will probably take on the Spirit of the context of when the Book of Life is mentioned.

WRESTLERS/CO-LABORERS

*Philippians 4:3, NKJV: And I urge you also, true companion, help these women who **labored (lit.; wrestled)** with me in the gospel, with Clement also, and the rest of my **fellow workers**, whose names are in **the Book of Life**.*

It is the "fellow workers" who are mentioned as being in the Book of Life. In other words, we must continue to "labor (wrestle) with" the apostles and all ministers "in the gospel." This will cause the apostle to bear witness of the precious truth that Saints are indeed "fellow workers…in the Book of Life." It is when the Saints wrestle with the apostles in the gospel that assurance of being in the Book of Life is highlighted by a foundation ministry of an apostle.

That is why there is so much skepticism in some in the Church as to who is in the Book of Life. Some are not "wrestling" in prayer and giving of finance with the apostles. Some are not fellow workers with the apostles. Thus, they are uncertain about their names being in the Book of Life.

In other words, lazy Christians are in a plight. They refuse to help the apostles; therefore, there is no apostolic confirmation in their lives. The apostle Paul and Clement found some fellow workers who were "wrestling" with them in the Gospel. Some were "women" (compare Luke 8:2-3).

If this were to happen today, they would call an apostle a womanizer. These things ought to stop. Every man of God is not interested in going to bed with Saints. There are apostles who are sincere, and they need help from praying women. Paul was also encouraging the Philippians to continue to do the work of the ministry toward him.

They were financially supporting him. Thus, they also were wrestling with him in the gospel. Their names were also in the Book of Life. To give you a brief lesson on understanding the Scripture, whatever is mentioned in an Epistle to a Church is usually personified in that Church. The Philippians are also in the Book of Life. They were a Church that overcame obstacles to give to Paul.

OVERCOME

*Revelation 3:5, NKJV: He who **overcomes** shall be clothed in white garments, and I will **not** blot out his name from **the Book of Life;** but I will confess his name before My Father and before His angels.*

The verse above was written to a Church named Sardis, which also points to any Church today that has the same pitfalls. Nonetheless, the Church of Sardis was told by the Lord that overcoming the state they were in was the only way to insure that their names would not be blotted out of the Book of Life. Yes, it is possible to get your name blotted out if you do not overcome.

In other words, once saved does not mean that you will always be saved. According to Jesus, this salvation is predicated on enduring to the end (Matthew 10:22), and as seen in the Scripture above, a name can be blotted out of the Book of Life. False prophets in Ezekiel's days also exemplified this. The false prophets' names were either deleted or not "written in the record...."

*Ezekiel 13:9, NKJV: My hand will be against the [false] prophets who envision futility and who divine lies; they shall not be in the assembly of My people, **nor be written in the record of the house of Israel,** nor shall they enter into the land of Israel. Then you shall know that I am the Lord GOD.*

These prophets prophesied lies. They also did not have the "foundation" of God's truth, because God eventually "uncovered" their foundation to their "disgrace" (Ezekiel 13:14). "Uncovered," used in Ezekiel 13:14, is defined in Strong's Lexicon as "to denude" (especially in a disgraceful sense).

Thus, because they did not maintain God's truth in their lives; and they did not really have the foundation of God words; they were "disgraced" and not "written in the record of the house of Israel." The Church of Sardis almost had their names removed from the Book of Life.

Without going into detail, the sin of Sardis was luxury that promoted complacency. Luxury apart from real relationship with God may make a Church or a person "have a name that you are alive, but you are dead" (Revelation 3:1, NKJV). "Sardis" is from the Greek word "sarx," which means (red) flesh. Thus, the Church at Sardis was probably flesh natured (Galatians 5:19-21).

*1 Timothy5:6, NKJV: But she who lives in **pleasure (lit.; luxury)** is **dead while she lives**.*

This is a serious thing, to appear to be alive, yet in reality be dead. Sardis has to overcome this oxymoron—alive, yet dead. According to the Word, the vices which are full of pleasure, which cause a state of living-dead are overcome by "watching" (Revelation 3:2). Paul also called this lack of watching (praying) a "living-dead" state.

In the case of the women that Paul addressed, the pleasure they were trapped in was the luxury of not trusting God and "continuing in supplications (asking for favor) and prayers night and day" (1 Timothy 5:5). Some Churches today are sleeping because of excessive luxury—no watching, no supplicating, no prayer. If Scripture interprets Scripture, and it does, then the sins of Sardis also include sexual sins. How is this?

The women discussed by Paul in Timothy were young widows who preferred sexuality to praying and supplicating. This exemplifies some Churches today. Some Churches (including males and females) choose luxury over watching, praying, and supplicating. Again, this luxurious, yet dead living is overcome by "watching."

This Church was warned to overcome, which is significant. If a name is blotted out of the Book of Life, the door is opened for beast worship. This is serious because the only ones who worship the beast and marvel at the beast are those who are not written in the Book of Life. Therefore, overcome by watching, in order not to worship the beast systems of the world.

DON'T MARVEL AT THE BEAST

*Revelation 13:8, NKJV: All who dwell on the earth will **worship** him [the beast], whose names have **not** been written in **the Book of Life of the Lamb** slain from the foundation of the world.*

*Revelation 17:8, NKJV: The beast that you saw was, and is not, and will ascend out of the bottomless pit and go to perdition. And those who dwell on the earth will **marvel**, whose names are **not** written in **the Book of Life** from the foundation of the world, when they see the beast that was, and is not, and yet is.*

Those who "worship" the world systems are not written in the Lamb's Book of Life. Saying it another way, if your name is not in the Book of Life, you will "worship" the beast. Saying it yet another way, if you "marvel" at the beast and its systems, this is because your name is not written in the Book of Life.

In other words, the fact that your name is written in the Book of Life, through faith in Jesus, you cannot and will not worship or marvel at the beast. You will not and cannot be marked with the beast's mark, name and/or number. This is good news. That is why a Christian should strive not to get his/her name blotted out of the Book of Life.

We have overcome and we must continue to overcome through faith in the Lamb of God. There will be a judgment for on those whose names are not written in the Lamb's Book of Life. Being "not found written in the Book of Life" can also come through one's name being "blotted out." "He who **overcomes**...I will **not** blot out his name from **the Book of Life**...." Let us continue to overcome.

ANOTHER BOOK

Revelation 20:12, NKJV: And I saw the dead, small and great, standing before God, and books were opened. And another book was opened, which is the Book of Life. And the dead were judged according to their works, by the things which were written in the books.

Revelation 20:15, NKJV: And anyone not found written in the Book of Life was cast into the lake of fire.

There are "books" and then there is "another book…which is the Book of Life." There are "books" with "things" written in their books. And there is "another book" with "names written in it. **All** had "things" written in the "book" **against** them. However, for some of those who had "things" written against them in the "books," the "things" were blotted out. Jesus has "**wiped out** the handwriting of requirements that was **against** us, which was contrary to us. And He has taken it out of the way, having nailed it to the cross" (Colossians 2:14, NKJV).

If a name was not in the Book of Life, the book of Revelation teaches that there is a **"section"** in the lake of fire designated for each person not found written in that book. God does not take pleasure in the death of the wicked (Ezekiel 33:11). He wants to "wipe out" the bad "things" in the books; and let the names of those who believe in the Lamb's sacrifices remain written in the Book of Life. However, He knew from the foundation of the world the ones who would **remain** written in the Book of Life.

False prophets will not remain written in the Book of Life (Ezekiel 13: 9). Any Church that does not overcome the oxymoron of "living-dead" is also a candidate for the lake of fire (Revelation 3:5). Idolatry of calf (the calf of Egypt, which is the religious image of the beastly world) will also cause one's name to be blotted out of the Book of Life (Exodus 32:32). Those who "take away from the words" of the book of Revelation will also **lose** their "part" in the Book of Life (Revelation 22:18-19). Death and Hades are not written in the Book of Life. They were cast into the lake of fire also.

There is a "book of remembrance" among these "books" with "things" written in them (Malachi 3:16). Let us also be a part of that book. It is my sincere desire that everyone (those who know their names are written in the Book of Life and those who do not yet know their names are written in the Book of Life may be able to enter in the City of God—New Jerusalem.

ENTER IN

*Revelation 21:27, NKJV: But there shall by no means **enter** it anything that defiles, or causes an abomination or a lie, but only those **who are written** in the Lamb's Book of Life.*

By way of reminder, for those who may read this chapter before reading the earlier chapters, the city—New Jerusalem—is the Church of the living God. We can only enter His Church by having our names written in the Book of Life. The writer of the book of Hebrews taught the same thing.

*Hebrews 12:22-23, NKJV: ²²**But you have come** to Mount Zion and to the city of the living God, the heavenly Jerusalem, to an innumerable company of angels, ²³to the general assembly and **church** of the firstborn who are **registered** in heaven, to God the Judge of all, to the spirits of just men made perfect.*

We "have come" to those "who are registered in heaven," now. We "have come to…the heavenly Jerusalem," now. Therefore, we can go into the city to worship and fellowship, and we can go out to evangelize. We enter in to be changed at the gates. Every gate is an experience that matures us, and we must go through each gate. This is a privilege.

We can go through the gates of the city because our names are written in the Book of Life. You may say, Brother Peart, I believe, yet I can't seem to enter in (mature in) the gates of the city. There is an answer for this lack of growth or lack of ability to enter the things of God. Let us look at Revelation 21:27 again:

*Revelation 21:27, NKJV: But there shall by no means **enter** it anything that **defiles**, or **causes** an **abomination** or a **lie**, but only those **who are written** in the Lamb's Book of Life.*

If you are a Christian, you must not continue to be one who "defiles." You must **not** cause an abomination (disgusting things, idols). If you are saved, you must **not** cause a lie (worshiping or reverencing creatures instead of God).

In other words, do not let people be more important to you in the place of God. These are some of the things that will hinder one's ability to enter in the City of God. In fact, Revelation 21:27 also implies that one's name being written in the Book of Life will cause hindrances to cease in one's life.

If it is indeed a fact that you have entered the Church of God through the "door" (Jesus), then you must be delivered from **causing defilement, causing abominations, causing lies**. The emphasis is **"causes"** or causation. We should not **cause** other people to feel the bondages of defilement. We should not cause others to do abominable things. We should not cause others to participate in the lie or tell lies. We are delivered from these things when we are allowed to walk through the first door or gate, which is Jesus. We are now the **"blessed"** and **causers** of blessings, through Jesus.

John said that the person who reads and hears the book of Revelation is automatically **"blessed"** (Revelation 1:3). This is why I cannot understand why men of God put this book off limits and put this book in the future. Those who take away from the book of Revelation will be removed from the Book of Life.

DO NOT TAKE AWAY

*Revelation 22:19, NKJV: And if anyone **takes away** from the words of the book of this prophecy, God shall **take away** his **part** from the Book of Life, from the holy city, and from the things which are written in this book.*

This is strong meat. Men of God have to be careful not to "take away" from the book of Revelation. We have no right to say that the book of Revelation is **only** for the future. The book of Revelation is also for the present. The book Revelation is a book about Jesus and His Church. We just have to learn how to understand the language. The language of the book of Revelation is the language of the Spirit. The book of Revelation was seen in the Spirit; and will be understood in the Spirit and by the Spirit.

*Revelation 1:10, NKJV: I was **in the Spirit** on the Lord's Day, and I heard behind me a loud voice, as of a trumpet.*

*1 Corinthians 2:13, NKJV: These things we also speak, not in words which man's wisdom teaches but which the **Holy Spirit teaches, comparing** spiritual things with spiritual.*

John saw the book of Revelation "in the Spirit." Thus, the book can only be understood through the "Spirit" "The Law [Word of God] is spiritual" (Romans 7:14a). The Holy Spirit is also "spiritual" (1 Corinthians 2:13). Thus, the book of Revelation can be understood in the Word of God through the revelation of the Holy Spirit. "The Holy Spirit teaches, comparing spiritual things to spiritual."

Thus, men of God should not take away something from the book of Revelation that they cannot understand. Taking away from the book of Revelation is treading on dangerous ground. Your "section" in the Book of Life[30] may be removed. I encourage the reader to conquer Book Town.

Be an overcoming Believer. Ensure that your name remains written in the Book of Life. The Holy Spirit is the "ink" that the Lamb uses to write you in the Book of Life. "Clearly you are an epistle written…with ink…by the Spirit of the living God… (2 Corinthians 3:3a).

---

[30] The Majority Texts and the Alexandrian Text reads "Tree of Life" in lieu of "the Book of Life."

THE LAMB, THE ONLY DYNASTY

1 Timothy 6:13-15, NKJV: *[13]I urge you in the sight of God who gives life to all things, and before Christ Jesus who witnessed the good confession before Pontius Pilate, [14]that you keep this commandment without spot, blameless until our Lord Jesus Christ's appearing, [15]which He will manifest in His own time, He who is the blessed and* **only Potentate (lit.; dynasty),** *the King of kings and Lord of lords.*

Revelation 17:13-14, NKJV: *[13]These are of one mind (lit.; opinion), and they will give their power and authority to the beast.* **[14]These will make war with the Lamb, and the Lamb will overcome them, for He is Lord of lords and King of kings;** *and those who are with Him are called, chosen, and faithful."*

Technically, the Lamb is **already** the "only Potentate" who exists. All other dominions visible and invisible were crushed by Him. The Lambkins just have to realize the victory and appropriate the dominion for the Church. "Jesus" is the one we "see" who has put all things under His feet (Hebrews 2:5-9; 1 Peter 3:22).

The Lamb will be the "only Potentate" under God (1 Corinthians 15:27) who will be standing when all rule has been put under Him, through the "feet" ministry of His Church (1 Corinthians 15:25-26). The Lamb has and will overcome the beast and the ten horns who agree to submit to the revitalized beast in the first[31] hour of the millennium.

---

[31] See my book, *The Last Hour, The First Hour, The Forty-second Generation.*

This beast (a continuation of the fourth kingdom and the four beast kingdom combined as depicted by Nebuchadnezzar and Daniel) will be different from the three dominions before it. The Lamb and His Lambkins ("those who are with Him") will eventually cause this regenerated fourth beast to crumble completely.

ONLY FOUR EARTHLY KINGDOMS

*Daniel 2:40, NKJV: And the **fourth** kingdom shall be as strong as iron, inasmuch as iron breaks in pieces and shatters everything; and like iron that crushes, that kingdom will break in pieces and crush all the others.*

*Daniel 7:2-3, NKJV: ²Daniel spoke, saying, "I saw in my vision by night, and behold, the four winds of heaven were stirring up the Great Sea. ³And **four** great **beasts** came up from the sea, each different from the other.*

The book of Daniel spoke about four earthly kingdoms in Daniel Chapter 2 and Daniel Chapter 7. In Daniel Chapter 2, Nebuchadnezzar was a heathen; even though he eventually got saved (turned from Babylon's gods to follow **the Most High God**). Nebuchadnezzar (a heathen) saw the **four** kingdoms as beautiful metals.

However, when a prophet (Daniel) saw these same kingdoms that would rule until Christ, Daniel saw them as nothing but beasts. Who is right, Nebuchadnezzar or Daniel? The answer is both are right.

The kingdoms of this world are both beautiful and beastly. In the political leaders' eyes their dominions are beautiful. However, in the eyes of a prophet the kingdoms of the world are but beasts. Why?

These beasts will devour human lives, ranging from the life of the Lamb to the poorest slaves. Jesus was indeed slain by a beast;

however, Jesus was resurrected by the power of God. The same stone that was rejected by the beast has become the chief cornerstone and this "cornerstone" will "grind him (the beast) to powder."

Nonetheless, the book of Daniel only mentioned **four** earthly kingdoms that would rise from the earth, and one heavenly Kingdom (the fifth) that would eventually destroy the four earthly kingdoms. The fifth kingdom is the kingdom of God. Let us read what Daniel said about the kingdoms of the earth.

Daniel 7:17-23, NKJV: ¹⁷*Those great beasts, which are four, are **four kings** which arise out of the earth….* ²³*the fourth beast shall be the **fourth kingdom** on earth.*

The right teaching concerning the kingdoms of the beasts is that there are only four earthly kingdoms mentioned in the Bible. Commentaries have added additional kingdoms arbitrarily. They are wrong. There are only four kingdoms to arise out of the earth. The error may have arisen out of trying to justify the apparent "other" kingdoms that existed after the Roman Empire.

Some scholars missed a key principle concerning the "fourth beast" (kingdom). This kingdom is "different" (Daniel 7:7) from the other beasts; and it is/will be "divided;" (Daniel 2:41) and it will have a plurality of "kings" at one time unlike the other kingdoms which only have one "king" per cycle (Daniel 2:44; Daniel 7:7, Revelation 17:12, etc., etc.). This fourth beast also duplicates (diversify, changes, revitalizes) itself into other forms through the ages (Daniel 7:7).

THE COLLISION

*Daniel 2:34, NKJV; You watched while a **stone** was cut out **without hands**, which **struck** the image on its **feet** of iron and clay and **broke** them in pieces.*

*Matthew 21:42-44, NKJV: 42Jesus said to them, "Have you never read in the Scriptures: 'The **stone** which the builders rejected has **become the chief cornerstone.** This was the LORD's doing, and it is marvelous in our eyes'? 43"Therefore I say to you, the kingdom of God will be taken from you and given to a nation bearing the fruits of it. 44 And whoever falls on this stone will be broken; but on whomever it [the stone] falls, it will **grind** him to **powder.**"*

There was a collision approximately two thousand years ago. The Lamb (the Stone) collided with the feet of the Roman Empire, and the stone crushed the feet of the empire. The encounter of Jesus with Pontius Pilate was a collision of the Stone with the feet (footprint) of Rome. The stone crushed the feet.

This is seen in the fact that after Pilate's (part of the feet (extension) of Rome) encounter with Jesus as Jesus witnessed a good confession concerning His Kingship. Pilate acknowledged that Jesus is indeed "King…" (John 19:19-22). This "acknowledgement" is a form of surrender to the conquering King—Jesus. In other words, the crumbling of the fourth kingdom began when Rome encountered and acknowledged King Jesus at the time of His crucifixion.

It also follows that as the Jews and the mobilized portion of Rome (the feet of Rome) rejected Jesus (the Stone), this same Stone "became the chief cornerstone." This same Stone also became a Stone that "grind…to powder" all whom He "falls on." Jesus and His Kingdom is the One who pulverized the image's feet in Daniel 2:34 w/2:44-45). It may not have been apparent to the natural eyes;

yet Jesus initiated Rome's termination as a world government. Any future empire (revived beast with its horns) will be fragile, divided and brief.

The crushing blow of the Stone will become apparent when the last part (the "gold") of that image in Daniel, Chapter 2 falls so all can "see" (compare Revelation 18:9). This gold is Babylon; and if you can receive it, the "broken gold" now applies to the "fallen" state of mystery Babylon (Revelation 17:5; Daniel 2:38; Daniel 2:45; Revelation 14:8; Revelation 18:2, and so on). When the "gold" falls the kingdom of the world will acknowledge what Jesus **already** accomplished (Revelation 11:15). Jesus **already** crushed the kingdoms of the world (visible and invisible).

In other words, the Stone of Daniel 2:34 started the demise of the fourth beast system. This Stone that eventually becomes a stone kingdom will eventually remove all the remnant of the first four kingdoms. And believe it or not, the demise started when Rome collided with the smitten Rock that eventually became the elevated Rock. The Rejected Stone has become the **"only** Potentate." The rejected Stone has become a ruling **mountain** ("Great Mountain") in the earth over sin, death and eventually all nations.

THE SMITTEN BECAME THE CRUSHER

*Daniel 2:35, NKJV: ... And the stone that **struck** the image became a great **mountain** and filled the whole earth.*

*Daniel 2:45, NKJV: Inasmuch as you saw that the **stone** was **cut out** of the **mountain** without hands, and that it **broke** in pieces the iron, the bronze, the clay, the silver, and the gold....*

The fourth kingdom has been crumbling for two thousand years. The destruction began with the death, burial, and resurrection of Jesus. This answer is given in the verses above. The Hebrew word for **"mountain"** used in the verses above is the same word used for the **"rock"** that was **smitten** by Moses.

*Exodus 17:6, NKJV: Behold, I will stand before you there on the rock in Horeb; and you shall **strike** the **rock**, and water will come out of it, that the people may drink." And Moses did so in the sight of the elders of Israel.*

Thus, "mountain" in Daniel 2:35 and Daniel 2:45 could be translated as "rock." The "stone" was cut out of a "rock;" but not just any rock. This was a Rock that was struck (crucified.) God commanded Moses to **"strike"** the Rock. Paul said in I Corinthians 10: 4 that that "Rock" was "Christ." Therefore, when Moses struck the rock the first time at God's command, it was a type of Christ being smitten on the cross for the nations.[32]

The "mountain" ("Rock") in Daniel 2:35 and 2:45 is the entity that tells us at what era the Stone struck the fourth beast. The Lamb of God struck the fourth kingdom when He was smitten during the crucifixion period. The fourth kingdom is **divided** and is being crumbled by the Rock's pounding.

The Rock, who was smitten, became the very Stone who crushed the feet of Rome. The destruction of Rome began before Rome was even aware of it. The Lamb defeated the beast two thousand years ago; and became the "only dynasty" that remains in the earth. Christianity caused Rome to crumble through the Lamb.

This was demonstrated when the empire of Rome became subjected to Christianity. The emperor of Rome, Constantine, in 313 AD established freedom of worship, because the gospel of God

---

[32] I learned this principle from the late Dr. Kelley Varner

had impacted his empire.[33] The rejected Stone, Jesus, became the "Chief-stone." Even in Rome that was previously violent against the Lamb and His lambkins. Therefore, Rome's subjection to the gospel eased the centuries of persecution against Christians. Rome also recognized Christianity as a legal body. In 391 A.D. Christianity became the official religion of Rome (although this "Romanized Church" has become a snare to humanity where manmade building are now called "churches" and the name "holy father" (the heavenly Father's name) is now assumed by men, and so on). The Lamb overcame Rome, and He is still overcoming the kingdoms of Satan and all its false religions associated with his kingdom. Thus, the fourth beast (the Roman Empire) eventually had to bow to the "only Potentate" — Jesus; and eventually the Stone kingdom (God's kingdom) will grow into a mountain that fills the entire earth.

KING OF KINGS, LORD OF LORDS

1 Timothy 6:13-15, NKJV: [13]*I urge you in the sight of God who gives life to all things, and before Christ Jesus who witnessed the good confession before Pontius Pilate,* [14]*that you keep this commandment without spot, blameless until our Lord Jesus Christ's appearing,* [15]*which He will manifest in His own time, He who is the blessed and* **only Potentate** **(lit.; dynasty),** *the King of kings and Lord of lords.*

The implication in the statement above is that a Potentate is considered a dynasty when a person is King of kings and Lord of

---

[33] Note: God meant the acceptance of Christianity for the good, generally speaking, giving them rest from persecution through Jesus' dominion; however, Constatine's acceptance of Christianity was also a ploy by him to unite his empire, utilizing the known demonstration of the Body of Christ's ability to incorporate races and nationalities, without prejudices, in the bond of love and peace.

lords. Jesus defeated all other dynasties. According to the Scriptures all the kingdoms of the world were under the enemy's authority until Jesus destroyed its dynasties.

*Acts 10:38, NKJV: How God anointed Jesus of Nazareth with the Holy Spirit and with power, who went about doing good and healing all who were **oppressed** by the devil, for God was with Him.*

*Matthew 4:8, NKJV: Again, the devil took Him up on an exceedingly high mountain and showed Him **all the kingdoms of the world** and their glory.*

A dynasty is a rule that has other kings subjugated to it. The Devil showed Jesus all the "kingdoms of the world," which he also said were "delivered" to him (Luke 4: 6). Peter in the book of Acts indicated that the Devil also **"had,"** and I stress **"had"** an "oppressive" dynasty.

"Oppressed" in Acts 10:38 is a compound of two Greek words ["kata" (down) and "dunastes" (dynasty)] which literally means to hold "down" someone or something with a "dynasty." Jesus reversed this on the devil. Jesus now "struck down" all dynasties of the enemy. Jesus is the only dynasty that exists now.

Jesus "has put down the mighty (lit.; dynasties) from their thrones…" (Luke 1:52). According to Paul in 1 Timothy Jesus is the **"only dynasty"** that remains. Paul made this statement relative to Pontus Pilate, an extension (the feet) of Rome—the fourth beast. The Stone (Jesus) crushed the dynasty of Rome. The devil does not have any more spiritual dynasty; and the fourth beast does not have any dynasty. The "only dynasty" is Jesus—the Lamb of God. He is King of kings and Lord of lords.

Being King of kings and Lord of lords is the truth that the revived beast is and will be utterly defeated by the Lamb and His lambkins.

The Church must realize her position relative to the rule of the nations. The Church and her children must understand the dynasty of the Lamb. Jesus — The Lamb is King, now. Jesus is Lord, now. To prove He has a dynasty, the stone has grown and is becoming that **"mountain"** that is filling the "whole earth" or "habitable world" (Daniel 2; Matthew 24:14).

Saying it another way, Jesus' Body (His called-out ones) has been growing and growing since Jesus established His Kingdom almost two thousand years ago. The Lamb's Kingdom grew so much that it is believed that one-half to three-quarters of the Roman Empire, a part of the fourth beast, were believers in the gospel of Jesus. The beast has tried to destroy the Lamb and His people; however, the dynasty remains and grows. Why? The Lamb is Lord of lords and King of kings.

Revelation 17:13-14, NKJV: [13]*These are of one mind (lit opinion), and they will give their power and authority to the beast.* [14]*These will make war with the Lamb, and the Lamb will overcome them,* ***for*** *He is* ***Lord*** *of lords and* ***King*** *of kings; and those who are with Him are called, chosen, and faithful."*

In reference to Jesus in the New Testament, the phrase King of kings and Lord of lords is used three times. Twice "King of kings" comes before "Lord of lords (1 Timothy 6:15, Revelation 19:16). The only time it is reversed to read "Lord of lords and King of kings" is in Revelation 17:14 cited above.

Jesus is "Lord" (lit.; Supreme Authority, Controller, Master, Sir, Mister). The Lord overcame and overcame the beast **"for"** He is Lord of lords, first; and the equal twin is He is "King of kings." He is Supreme over the Satan, the corporate Satan, the beast, the other beast, the false prophet, "et. al." The Lamb is the master of the beast and its system. He is the **controller** of the beast. Thus, God is controlling the beast to "fulfill His purpose."

*Revelation 17:17, NKJV For God has put it into their hearts to **fulfill His purpose,** to be of one mind, and to give their kingdom to the beast, **until the words of God are fulfilled.***

God is using the beast to "fulfill" His word. Yet, the beast, as his nature is, will make war on the Lamb by being irrational. The Assyrians did the same things. God used them to fulfill his words (Isaiah 10:5-7). The Assyrians then became prideful against God and the natural Jews (compare Isaiah 10:7 with Isaiah 10:12 and 10:15). Thus, God had to put down the rule of the Assyrians (Isaiah 10:24-27).

As God punished the Assyrians, the Lamb will destroy the beast. The beast will exercise war on the Saints—the spiritual Jews (Revelation 13:7). The war against the Lamb and the lambkins will be last war he ever makes. The Lamb, who is the **"only Potentate,"** will overcome the beast. The beast will be "arrested," cast into the lake of fire and lightning; **"for"** Jesus is the "only dynasty." Yes! Jesus is Lord! Amen!

Revelation 19:11-20, NKJV: [11]*Now I saw heaven opened, and behold, a white horse. And He who sat on him was called Faithful and True, and in righteousness He judges and makes **war**...*[16]*And He has on His robe and on His thigh a name written: KING OF KINGS AND LORD OF LORDS...*[19]*And I saw the beast, the kings of the earth, and their armies, gathered together to make **war** against Him who sat on the horse and against His army.* [20]*Then the beast was captured, and with him the false prophet ... These two were cast alive into the lake of fire burning with brimstone.*

The Lord is unconquerable. Jesus **is** both King and Lord! He is the **"only Potentate"** who remains.

OTHER BOOKS

Wisdom from Above, by Judith Peart
Procreation, Understanding Sex and Identity by Judith Peart
100 Nevers, by Judith Peart
The Shattered and the Healing by Judith Peart
The Lamb, by Donald Peart
Jesus' Resurrection, Our Inheritance, by Donald Peart.
Sexuality, By Donald Peart
Forgiven 490 Times, by Donald Peart w/Judith Peart!
The Days of the Seventh Angel, By Donald Peart
The Torah (The Principle) of Giving, by Donald Peart
The Time Came, by Donald Peart
The Last Hour, the First Hour, the Forty-Second Generation, by Donald Peart
Vision Real, by Donald Peart
The False Prophet, Alias, Another Beast V1, by Donald Peart
"the beast," by Donald Peart
Son of Man Prophesy Against the false prophet, by Donald Peart
The Many False Prophets (The Dragon's Tail), by Donald Peart
The Work of Lawlessness Revealed, by Donald Peart
When the Lord Made the Tempter, by Donald Peart
Examining Doctrine, Volume 1, by Donald Peart
Exousia, Your God Given Authority, by Donald Peart
The Numbers of God, by Donald Peart
The Completions of the Ages … by Donald Peart
The Revelation of Jesus Christ, by Donald Peart
Jude—Translation and Commentary, by Donald Peart
Obtaining the Better Resurrection, by Donald Peart
Manifestations from Our Lord Jesus …by Donald and Judith Peart).
Obtaining the Better Resurrection, by Donald Peart
The New Testament, Dr. Donald Peart Exegesis
The Tree of Life, By Dr. Donald Peart
The Spirit and Power of John, the Baptist by Dr. Donald Peart
The Shattered and the Healing by Judith Peart
Is She Married to a Husband? by Donald Peart
The Ugliest Man God Made by Donald Peart
Does Answering the Call of God Impact Your Children? by Donald Peart
Victory Out-of-the Beast-the Harvest of the Earth by Donald Peart
The Order of Melchizedek by Donald Peart
Ezekiel-the House-the City-the Land (Interpreting the Patterns) by Donald Peart

Contact Information:
Crown of Glory Ministries
P.O. Box 1041 Randallstown, MD 21133
donaldpeart7@gmail.com

www.ingramcontent.com/pod-product-compliance
Lightning Source LLC
Chambersburg PA
CBHW032106090426
42743CB00007B/261